Georgia
PhysicalScience
EOC
SUCCESS STRATEGIES

Georgia EOC Test Review for the Georgia End of Course Tests

Dear Future Exam Success Story:

Congratulations on your purchase of our study guide. Our goal in writing our study guide was to cover the content on the test, as well as provide insight into typical test taking mistakes and how to overcome them.

Standardized tests are a key component of being successful, which only increases the importance of doing well in the high-pressure high-stakes environment of test day. How well you do on this test will have a significant impact on your future, and we have the research and practical advice to help you execute on test day.

The product you're reading now is designed to exploit weaknesses in the test itself, and help you avoid the most common errors test takers frequently make.

How to use this study guide

We don't want to waste your time. Our study guide is fast-paced and fluff-free. We suggest going through it a number of times, as repetition is an important part of learning new information and concepts.

First, read through the study guide completely to get a feel for the content and organization. Read the general success strategies first, and then proceed to the content sections. Each tip has been carefully selected for its effectiveness.

Second, read through the study guide again, and take notes in the margins and highlight those sections where you may have a particular weakness.

Finally, bring the manual with you on test day and study it before the exam begins.

Your success is our success

We would be delighted to hear about your success. Send us an email and tell us your story. Thanks for your business and we wish you continued success.

Sincerely,

Mometrix Test Preparation Team

Need more help? Check out our flashcards at: http://MometrixFlashcards.com/Georgia

Written and edited by the Mometrix Exam Secrets Test Prep Team
Printed in the United States of America

TABLE OF CONTENTS

Top 20 Test Taking Tips

1. Carefully follow all the test registration procedures
2. Know the test directions, duration, topics, question types, how many questions
3. Setup a flexible study schedule at least 3-4 weeks before test day
4. Study during the time of day you are most alert, relaxed, and stress free
5. Maximize your learning style; visual learner use visual study aids, auditory learner use auditory study aids
6. Focus on your weakest knowledge base
7. Find a study partner to review with and help clarify questions
8. Practice, practice, practice
9. Get a good night's sleep; don't try to cram the night before the test
10. Eat a well balanced meal
11. Know the exact physical location of the testing site; drive the route to the site prior to test day
12. Bring a set of ear plugs; the testing center could be noisy
13. Wear comfortable, loose fitting, layered clothing to the testing center; prepare for it to be either cold or hot during the test
14. Bring at least 2 current forms of ID to the testing center
15. Arrive to the test early; be prepared to wait and be patient
16. Eliminate the obviously wrong answer choices, then guess the first remaining choice
17. Pace yourself; don't rush, but keep working and move on if you get stuck
18. Maintain a positive attitude even if the test is going poorly
19. Keep your first answer unless you are positive it is wrong
20. Check your work, don't make a careless mistake

Atomic and Nuclear Theory and the Periodic Table

Pure substances

Pure substances are substances that cannot be further broken down into simpler substances and still retain their characteristics. Pure substances are categorized as either elements or compounds. Elements that consist of only one type of atom may be monatomic, diatomic, or polyatomic. For example, helium (He) and copper (Cu) are monatomic elements, and hydrogen (H_2) and oxygen (O_2) are diatomic elements. Phosphorus (P_4) and sulfur (S_8) are polyatomic elements. Compounds consist of molecules of more than one type of atom. For example, pure water (H_2O) is made up of molecules consisting of two atoms of hydrogen bonded to one atom of oxygen, and glucose ($C_6H_{12}O_6$) is made up of molecules of six carbon atoms and twelve hydrogen atoms bonded together with six oxygen atoms.

Mixtures

Mixtures can be classified as either homogeneous mixtures or heterogeneous mixtures. The molecules of homogeneous mixtures are distributed uniformly throughout the mixture, but the molecules of heterogeneous mixtures are not distributed uniformly throughout the mixture. Air is an example of a homogeneous mixture, and a pile of sand and salt is an example of a heterogeneous mixture. Solutions are homogeneous mixtures consisting of a solute, the substance that is dissolved, and a solvent, the substance doing the dissolving. Examples of solutions include vinegar (a solution of acetic acid in water) and sugar dissolved in water. Suspensions are heterogeneous mixtures in which the particle size of the substance suspended is too large to be kept in suspension by Brownian motion. Once left undisturbed, suspensions will settle out to form layers. An example of a suspension is sand stirred into water. Left undisturbed, the sand will fall out of suspension and the water will form a layer on top of the sand.

States of matter

The four states of matter are solids, liquids, gases, and plasma. Solids have a definite shape and a definite volume. Because solid particles are held in fairly rigid positions, solids are the least compressible of the four states of matter. Liquids have definite volumes but no definite shapes. Because their particles are free to slip and slide over each other, liquids take the shape of their containers, but they still remain fairly incompressible by natural means. Gases have no definite shape or volume. Because gas particles are free to move, they move away from each other causing gases to fill their containers. This also makes gases very compressible. Plasmas are high-temperature, ionized gases that exist only under very high temperatures at which electrons are stripped away from their atoms.

Atoms and ions

Neutral atoms have equal numbers of protons and electrons. Some atoms tend to lose electrons in order to have a full outer shell of valence electrons and become positively charged ions or cations. For example, the alkali metals sodium and potassium form the cations Na^+ and K^+, and the alkaline earth metals magnesium and calcium form the cations Mg^{2+} and Ca^{2+}. Some atoms tend to gain electrons to fill their outer shells and become negatively charged ions or anions. For example, the halogens fluorine and chlorine form the anions F^- and Cl^-, and the chalcogens oxygen and sulfur form the anions O^{2-} and S^{2-}

Atoms and molecules

Atoms are the smallest particles of an element that still retain the properties of that element. For example, a copper atom is the smallest piece of a copper wire that still has the properties of copper. Molecules are made of two or more atoms. Molecules are the smallest particles of a compound that still retain the properties of that compound. For example, the substance water consists of water molecules of two hydrogen atoms covalently bonded to one oxygen atom. A water molecule is the smallest particle of water that still has the properties of water. Also, elements may be diatomic or polyatomic molecules. For example, hydrogen gas (H_2) exists naturally as diatomic molecules. In this case, the molecule could be further broken down into individual hydrogen atoms.

Chemical and physical properties

Matter has both physical and chemical properties. Physical properties can be seen or observed without changing the identity or composition of matter. For example, the mass, volume, and density of a substance can be determined without permanently changing the sample. Other physical properties include color, boiling point, freezing point, solubility, odor, hardness, electrical conductivity, thermal conductivity, ductility, and malleability. Chemical properties cannot be measured without changing the identity or composition of matter. Chemical properties describe how a substance reacts or changes to form a new substance. Examples of chemical properties include flammability, corrosivity, oxidation states, enthalpy of formation, and reactivity with other chemicals.

Chemical and physical changes

Physical changes do not produce new substances. The atoms or molecules may be rearranged, but no new substances are formed. Phase changes or changes of state such as melting, freezing, and sublimation are physical changes. For example, physical changes include the melting of ice, the boiling of water, sugar dissolving into water, and the crushing of a piece of chalk into a fine powder. Chemical changes involve a chemical reaction and do produce new substances. When iron rusts, iron oxide is formed, indicating a chemical change. Other examples of chemical changes include baking a cake, burning wood, digesting a cracker, and mixing an acid and a base.

Intensive and extensive properties

Physical properties are categorized as either intensive or extensive. Intensive properties *do not* depend on the amount of matter or quantity of the sample. This means that intensive properties will not change if the sample size is increased or decreased. Intensive properties include color, hardness, melting point, boiling point, density, ductility, malleability, specific heat, temperature, concentration, and magnetization. Extensive properties *do* depend on the amount of matter or quantity of the sample. Therefore, extensive properties do change if the sample size is increased or decreased. If the sample size is increased, the property increases. If the sample size is decreased, the property decreases. Extensive properties include volume, mass, weight, energy, entropy, number of moles, and electrical charge.

Law of conservation of mass

The law of conservation of mass is also known as the law of conservation of matter. This basically means that in a closed system, the total mass of the products must equal the total mass of the reactants. This could also be stated that in a closed system, mass never changes. A consequence of this law is that matter is never created or destroyed during a typical chemical reaction. The atoms of the reactants are simply rearranged to form the products. The number and type of each specific atom involved in the reactants is identical to the number and type of atoms in the products. This is the key principle used when balancing chemical equations. In a balanced chemical equation, the number of moles of each element on the reactant side equals the number of moles of each element on the product side.

Phase diagram and critical point

A phase diagram is a graph or chart of pressure versus temperature that represents the solid, liquid, and gaseous phases of a substance and the transitions between these phases. Typically, pressure is located on the vertical axis, and temperature is located along the horizontal axis. The curves drawn on the graph represent points at which different phases are in an equilibrium state. These curves indicate at which pressure and temperature the phase changes of sublimation, melting, and boiling occur. Specifically, the curve between the liquid and gas phases indicates the pressures and temperatures at which the liquid and gas phases are in equilibrium. The curve between the solid and liquid phases indicates the temperatures and pressures at which the solid and liquid phases are in equilibrium. The open spaces on the graph represent the distinct phases solid, liquid, and gas. The point on the curve at which the graph splits is referred to as the *critical point.* At the critical point, the solid, liquid, and gas phases all exist in a state of equilibrium.

Explanation of the lettered regions of a phase diagram

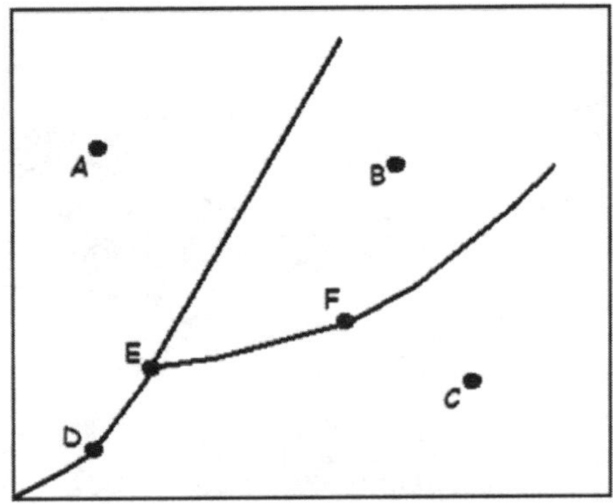

A—Solid phase: This is a region of high pressure and low temperature where the substance always exists as a solid.

B—Liquid phase: This is a region of pressure and temperature where the substance is in the liquid phase

C—Gas phase: This is a region of pressure and temperature where the substance is in the gaseous phase.

D—Sublimation point: The portion of the curve that contains point D shows all the combinations of pressure and temperature at which the solid phase is in equilibrium with the gaseous phase.

E—Critical point: The point at which the solid, liquid, and gaseous phases are all in equilibrium.

F—Boiling point: The line that contains point F indicates all the combinations of pressure and temperature at which the liquid phase and gas phase are in equilibrium.

Heat of vaporization, heat of fusion, and heat of sublimation

The *heat of vaporization* (ΔH_{vap}) is the amount of heat that must be added to one mole of a substance to change the substance from the liquid phase to the gaseous phase.

The *heat of fusion* (ΔH_{fus}) is the amount of heat that must be added to one mole of a substance to change the substance from the solid phase to the liquid phase.

The *heat of sublimation* (ΔH_{sub}) is the amount of heat that must be added to one mole of a substance to change the substance directly from the solid phase to the gaseous phase without passing through the liquid phase.

Calculate the amount of heat required to change 100.0 g of ice at –10.0 °C to water at 10.0 °C. (ΔH_{fus} = 334 J/g; c_{water} = 4.18 J/(g⍰°C), c_{ice} = 2.06 J/(g⍰°C)).

To calculate the amount of heat required to change 100.0 g of ice at –10.0 °C to water at 10.0 °C, it is necessary to calculate the heat required each step along the way. Step 1 is to calculate the heat required to raise the temperature of the ice from –10.0 °C to 0.0 °C. Step 2 is to calculate the amount of heat required to melt the ice. Finally, step 3 is to calculate the amount of heat required to raise the temperature of the water from 0.0 °C to 10.0 °C. For steps 1 and 3, the required equation is $Q = mc\Delta T$. Because step 2 is a phase change, the required equation is $Q = m\Delta H_{fus}$. For step 1: Q_1 = (100.0 g)(2.06 J/(g·°C))(0.0 °C – (–10.0 °C)) = 2,060 J. For step 2: $Q_2 = m\Delta H_{fus}$ = (100.0 g)(334 J/g) = 33,400 J. For step 3: Q_1 = (100.0 g)(4.18 J/(g·°C))(10.0 °C – 0.0 °C) = 4,180 J. Adding $Q_1 + Q_2 + Q_3$ = 2,060 J + 33,400 J + 4,180 J = 39,640 J.

Calculate the amount of heat required to change 100.0 g of water at 90.0 °C to steam at 110.0 °C (ΔH_{vap} = 2,260 J/g; c_{steam} = 1.86 J/(g⍰°C), c_{water} = 4.18 J/(g⍰°C)).

To calculate the amount of heat required to change 100.0 g of water at 90.0 °C to steam at 110.0 °C, it is necessary to calculate the heat required at each step along the way. Step 1 is to calculate the heat required to raise the temperature of the water from 90.0 °C to 100.0 °C. Step 2 is to calculate the amount of heat required to change the water to steam. Finally, step 3 is to calculate the amount of heat required to raise the temperature of the steam from 100.0 °C to 110.0 °C. For steps 1 and 3, the required equation is $Q = mc\Delta T$. Because Step 2 is a phase change, the required equation is $Q = m\Delta H_{vap}$. For step 1: Q_1 = (100.0 g)(4.18 J/(g·°C))(100.0 °C – 90.0 °C) = 4,180 J. For step 2: $Q_2 = m\Delta H_{vap}$ = (100.0 g)(2,260 J/g) = 226,000 J. For step 3: Q_1 = (100.0 g)(1.86 J/(g·°C))(110.0 °C – 100.0 °C) = 1,860 J. Adding $Q_1 + Q_2 + Q_3$ = 4,180 J + 226,000 J + 1,860 J = 233,040 J.

Sketch and describe the heating curve of water from –10 °C to 110 °C.

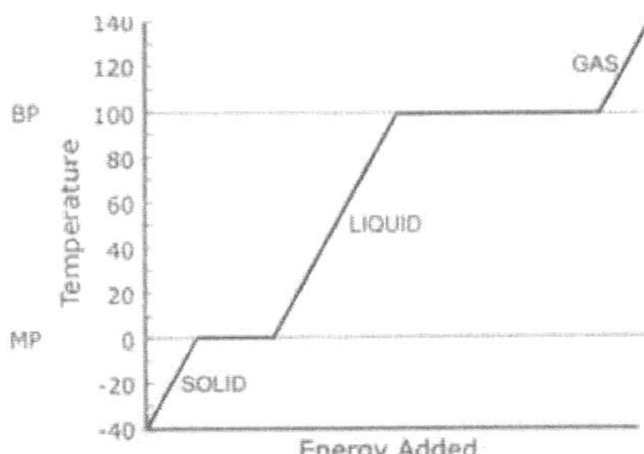

In the first portion of the curve, the graph slants up and to the right as the ice is a solid that is increasing in temperature from –10 °C to 0 °C. In the second portion of the curve, the graph remains horizontal during the phase change from solid to liquid as the temperature remains constant at 0 °C. In the third portion of the curve, the graph slants up and to the right as the water now is in the liquid state and is increasing in temperature from 0 °C to 100 °C. In the fourth portion of the curve, the graph remains horizontal during the phase change from liquid to gas as the temperature remains at 100 °C. In the last portion of the curve, the graph slants up and to the right as water now is the gaseous state and the steam is increasing in temperature from 100 °C to 110 °C.

Assumptions of the kinetic molecular theory

The kinetic molecular theory consists of several assumptions including the following:

1. Ideal gas molecules are in constant random motion. The gas molecules travel in straight lines until they collide with other gas molecules or with the walls of the container.
2. Ideal gas molecules have a negligible volume compared to the volume of the gas itself. Most of the volume of a gas is empty space.
3. Ideal gas molecules exert no attractive or repulsive forces on each other.
4. Ideal gas molecules have a kinetic energy that is directly proportional to the absolute temperature. The higher the temperature, the higher the average kinetic energy of the gas molecules, and the faster the gas molecules are moving.
5. Ideal gas molecules have perfectly elastic collisions. The kinetic energy lost by one gas molecule is gained by another gas molecule. No energy is lost in the collision with the container.

Ideal gases

An ideal gas is a hypothetical or theoretical gas. Ideal gases are assumed to be a set of randomly moving point particles that do not interact with each other. The collisions of ideal gases are assumed to be completely elastic, and the intermolecular forces are assumed to be zero. Real gases show more complex behaviors. The ideal gas laws tend to fail at low temperatures and high pressures when the effects of the particle size and intermolecular forces are more apparent. Also, the idea gas assumptions do not account for phase transitions.

Ideal gas law

The ideal gas law combines Boyle's law, Charles's law, and Avogadro's law. According to Boyle's law, $V \propto \frac{1}{P}$. According to Charles's law, $V \propto T$. According to Avogadro's law, $V \propto n$. Combining these three relationships into one relationship yields $V \propto \frac{nT}{P}$. Multiplying through by P yields $PV \propto nT$, or

$PV = nRT$, where R is the ideal gas constant of 0.0821 L·atm/(K·mol), P is the pressure in atm, V is the volume in L, n is the number of moles in mol, and T is the temperature in K.

Boyle's law

Boyle's law describes the relationship between the volume and pressure of an ideal gas at a constant temperature for a given amount of gas. For an ideal gas, volume and pressure are inversely related. Because gases are compressible, if the pressure of a gas sample is increased, the volume will decrease. If the pressure of a gas sample is decreased, the volume will increase. Conversely, if the volume of a gas sample is increased, the pressure will decrease. If the volume of a gas sample is decreased, the pressure will increase. For example, if the pressure of a gas sample is doubled, the volume decreases to one-half of the original volume. If the pressure of a gas sample is tripled, the volume decreases to one-third of the original volume. The relationship between volume and pressure is represented by $V \propto \frac{1}{P}$ or $V = k\frac{1}{P}$ or $PV = k$. Because the product of the pressure and the volume is a constant, Boyle's law can be stated as $P_iV_i = P_fV_f$.

Charles's law

Charles's law describes the relationship between the volume and temperature of an ideal gas at a constant pressure for a given amount of gas. For an ideal gas, volume and temperature are directly related. Because the kinetic energy of a gas is directly proportional to the absolute temperature, if the temperature increases, the average kinetic energy of the gas molecules increases. As the molecules move faster, they spread farther apart, increasing the volume. If the volume of the container is increased, the temperature will also increase due to the fact the molecules will have to move faster to strike the container more often because the pressure must remain constant. The relationship between volume and pressure is represented by $V \propto T$ or $V = kT$ or $\frac{V}{T} = k$. Because the quotient of the volume and the temperature is a constant, Charles's law can be stated as $\frac{V_i}{T_i} = \frac{V_f}{T_f}$, where the temperature is stated in kelvin.

Combined gas law

The combined gas law combines Boyle's law and Charles's law. According to Boyle's law, volume and pressure are inversely related, or $V \propto \frac{1}{P}$. According to Charles's law, volume and temperature are directly related, or $V \propto T$. Combining these relationships into one yields $V \propto \frac{T}{P}$ or $V = k\frac{T}{P}$.

Solving for k yields $\frac{PV}{T}$. Because $k = \frac{P_1V_1}{T_1}$ and $k = \frac{P_2V_2}{T_2}$, the combined gas law can be written as $\frac{P_1V_1}{T_1} = \frac{P_2V_2}{T_2}$. For situations in which $V_1 = V_2$, the combined gas law yields a relationship of $P \propto T$, indicating that for a constant volume, the pressure and temperature are directly related.

Avogadro's law

Avogadro's law describes the relationship between the volume and amount in moles of an ideal gas at a constant pressure and temperature. For an ideal gas, the volume and the number of moles are directly related. If the volume increases, the number of moles would have to increase in order to maintain the pressure and temperature. If the number of moles in the container increases, the volume will also need to increase to maintain the same pressure and temperature. The relationship between volume and amount in mole of a gas is represented by $V \propto N, V = kN$, or $\frac{V}{N} = k$. Because the quotient of the volume and the amount in moles is a constant, Avogadro's law can be stated as $\frac{V_i}{N_i} = \frac{V_f}{N_f}$.

Behavior of real gases

Although assuming that gases are ideal is appropriate for many situations, real gases behave differently than ideal gases. The collisions of real gases are not elastic. Real gases do have attractive and repulsive forces. Real gases have mass, whereas ideal gases do not. The atoms or molecules of real gases are not point particles, and they do interact with each other especially under high pressures and low temperatures. Under the right conditions of pressure and temperature, real gases will undergo phase transitions and become liquids. The pressure of real gases is less than those of ideal gases due to the small attractive forces between the particles in the gases.

Problem #1

A 5.0 L gas sample has a pressure of 1.0 standard atmosphere (atm). If the pressure is increased to 2.0 atm, find the new volume. Assume that the temperature is constant.

To find the new volume, use the equation associated with Boyle's law $P_iV_i = P_fV_f$. Solving the equation for the unknown V_f yields $V_f = \frac{P_iV_i}{P_f}$. Substituting in the given values $P_i = 1.0$ atm, $V_i = 5.0$ L, and $P_f = 2.0$ atm into the equation yields $V_f = \frac{(1.0 \text{ atm})(5.0 \text{ L})}{(2.0 \text{ atm})} = 2.5$ L. This checks because the pressure increased and the volume decreased. More specifically, because the pressure was doubled, the volume was reduced to one-half of the original volume.

Problem #2

A gas sample has a volume of 10.0 L at 200.0 K. Find its volume if the temperature is increased to 300.0 K.

To find the new volume, use the equation associated with Charles's law $\frac{V_i}{T_i} = \frac{V_f}{T_f}$. Solving the equation for the unknown V_f yields $V_f = \frac{T_fV_i}{T_i}$. Substituting the given values $V_i = 10.0$ L, $T_i = 200.0$ K, and $T_f = 300.0$ K into the equation yields $V_f = \frac{(300.0 \text{ K})(10.0 \text{ L})}{(200.0 \text{ K})} = 15.0$ L. This checks because the temperature increased and the volume increased. Also, note that if the temperature had not been stated in kelvin, it would have to be converted to kelvin before substituting the values in to the equation.

Problem #3

Find the pressure that 0.500 mol of H_2 (g) will exert on a 500.0 mL flask at 300.0 K.

To calculate the pressure that 0.500 mol of H_2 will exert on a 500.0 mL flask at 300.0 K, use the ideal gas equation $PV = nRT$, where R is the ideal gas constant of 0.0821 L·atm/(K·mol), P is the pressure in atm, V is the volume in L, n is the number of moles in mol, and T is the temperature in kelvin. Solving the ideal gas equation for P yields $P = \frac{nRT}{V}$. First, convert the 500.0 mL to 0.500 L. Substituting in n = 0.500 mol, V = 0.500 L, T = 300.0 K, and $R = 0.0821\,\frac{\text{L·atm}}{\text{K·mol}}$ yields $P = \frac{(0.500\text{ mol})(0.0821\text{ L·atm/(K·mol)}(300.0\text{ K})}{(0.500\text{ L})} = 24.6\text{ atm}$.

Subatomic particles

The three major subatomic particles are the proton, neutron, and electron. The proton, which is located in the nucleus, has a relative charge of +1. The neutron, which is located in the nucleus, has a relative charge of 0. The electron, which is located outside the nucleus, has a relative charge of −1. The proton and neutron, which are essentially the same mass, are much more massive than the electron and make up the mass of the atom. The electron's mass is insignificant compared to the mass of the proton and neutron.

Quantum numbers

The principal quantum number (n) describes an electron's shell or energy level and actually describes the size of the orbital. Electrons farther from the nucleus are at higher energy levels. The subshell or azimuthal quantum number (l) describes the electron's sublevel or subshell (*s, p, d,* or *f*) and specifies the shape of the orbital. Typical shapes include spherical, dumbbell, and clover leaf. The magnetic quantum number (m_l) describes the orientation of the orbital in space. The spin or magnetic moment quantum number (m_s) describes the direction of the spin of the electron in the orbital.

Orbits and orbitals

An orbit is a definite path, but an orbital is a region in space. The Bohr model described electrons as orbiting or following a definite path in space around the nucleus of an atom. But, according to the uncertainty principle, it is impossible to determine the location and the momentum of an electron simultaneously. Therefore, it is impossible to draw a definite path or orbit of an electron. An orbital as described by the quantum-mechanical model or the electron-cloud model is a region in space that is drawn in such a way as to indicate the probability of finding an electron at a specific location. The distance an orbital is located from the nucleus corresponds to the principal quantum number. The orbital shape corresponds to the subshell or azimuthal quantum number. The orbital orientation corresponds to the magnetic quantum number.

Cathode ray tube (CRT)

Electrons were discovered by Joseph John Thomson through scientific work with CRTs. Cathode rays had been studied for many years, but it was Thomson who showed that cathode rays were negatively charged particles. Although Thomson could not determine an electron's charge or mass, he was able to determine the ratio of the charge to the mass. Thomson discovered that this ratio was constant regardless of the gas in the CRT. He was able to show that the cathode rays were actually streams of negatively charged particles by deflecting them with a positively charged plate.

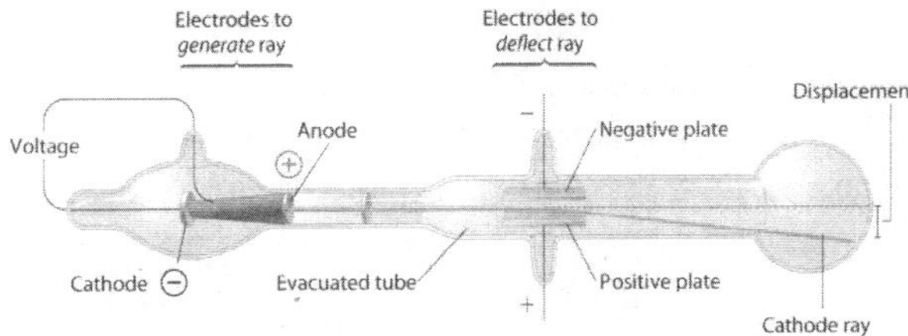

Gold foil experiment

After Thomson determined the ratio of the charge to the mass of an electron from studying cathode rays, he proposed the plum pudding model, in which he compared electrons to the raisins embedded in plum pudding. This model of the atom was disproved by the gold foil experiment. The gold foil experiment led to the discovery of the nucleus of an atom. Scientists at Rutherford's laboratory bombarded a thin gold foil with high-speed helium ions. Much to their surprise, some of the ions were reflected by the foil. The scientists concluded that the atom has a hard central core, which we now know to be the nucleus.

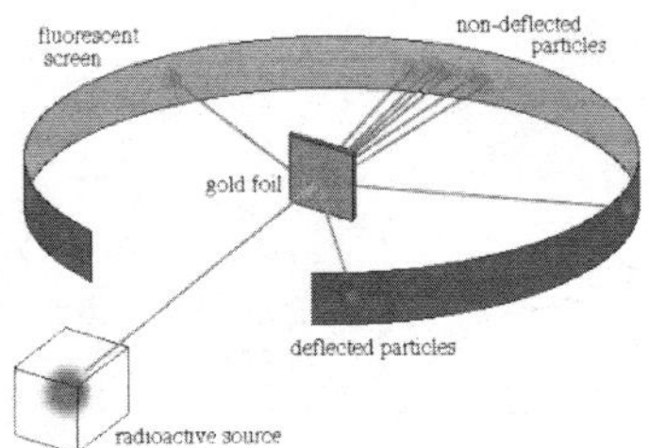

Problems that Rutherford's model had with spectral lines

Rutherford's model allowed for the electrons of an atom to be in an infinite number of orbits based on Newton's laws of motion. Rutherford believed that electrons could orbit the nucleus at any distance from the nucleus and that electrons could change velocity and direction at any moment. But, according to Rutherford's model, the electrons would lose energy and spiral into the nucleus. Unfortunately, if this was in fact true, then every atom would be unstable. Rutherford's model also does not correspond to the spectral lines emitted from gases at low pressure. The spectral lines are discrete bands of light at specific energy levels. These spectral lines indicate that electrons must be at specific distances from the nucleus. If electrons could be located at any distance from the nucleus, then these gases should emit continuous spectra instead of spectral lines.

Atomic number and mass number

The atomic number of an element is the number of protons in the nucleus of an atom of that element. This is the number that identifies the type of an atom. For example, all oxygen atoms have eight protons, and all carbon atoms have six protons. Each element is identified by its specific atomic number. The mass number is the number of protons and neutrons in the nucleus of an atom. Although the atomic number is the same for all atoms of a specific element, the mass number can vary due to the varying numbers of neutrons in various isotopes of the atom.

Isotope

Isotopes are atoms of the same element that vary in their number of neutrons. Isotopes of the same element have the same number of protons and thus the same atomic number. But, because isotopes vary in the number of neutrons, they can be identified by their mass numbers. For example, two naturally occurring carbon isotopes are carbon-12 and carbon-13, which have mass numbers 12 and 13, respectively. The symbols $^{12}_{6}C$ and $^{13}_{6}C$ also represent the carbon isotopes. The general form of the symbol is $^{M}_{A}X$, where X represents the element symbol, M represents the mass number, and A represents the atomic number.

Average atomic mass

The *average atomic mass* is the weighted average of the masses of all the naturally occurring isotopes of an atom in comparison to the carbon-12 isotope. The unit for average atomic mass is the atomic mass unit (u). Atomic masses of isotopes are measured using a mass spectrometer by bombarding a gaseous sample of the isotope and measuring its relative deflections. Atomic masses can be calculated if the percent abundances and the atomic masses of the naturally occurring isotopes are known.

Alpha particles

Alpha particles are the products of alpha decay. They are identical to helium nuclei. Alpha particles consist of two protons and two neutrons. Because they have two protons but zero electrons, alpha particles have a net +2 charge. They are represented by the Greek letter alpha as α, α^{2+}, or $^{4}_{2}\alpha^{2+}$. Because they are identical to helium nuclei, they may also be written as He^{2+}, $^{4}_{2}He$, or $^{4}_{2}He^{2+}$. Because alpha particles have a strong charge and travel slowly, they interact significantly with matter that they pass through and may therefore be stopped by a sheet of paper or a few inches of air. Alpha particles cannot penetrate the skin.

Beta particles

Beta particles are the products of beta decay. Beta particles may be high-speed electrons or high-speed positrons. These two forms of beta decay are designated by the Greek letter beta as β^- and β^+ or $_{-1}^{0}e$ and $_{+1}^{0}e$, respectively. Negative beta particles are created during radioactive decay when a neutron changes into a proton and an electron. Positive beta particles are created when a proton changes into a neutron and a positron. Beta particles have a greater penetrating ability than alpha particles. Beta particles can be stopped by thin plywood or metal or several feet of air.

Gamma radiation

Gamma radiation (represented by the Greek letter gamma, γ) is released during gamma decay. Often, atoms that have just undergone alpha or beta decay then undergo gamma decay. An atom produced during alpha or beta decay may still be in an excited state. The atom then releases this energy in a burst of gamma rays as high-energy photons. Gamma radiation is part of the electromagnetic spectrum and consists of electromagnetic waves that travel at the speed of light with frequencies higher than x-rays. Because gamma radiation has no charge, it easily penetrates solid substances. Gamma decay is useful in medical procedures, including cancer treatment.

Radioactive decay and half-life

Radioactivity or radioactive decay occurs when an unstable atom splits to form a more stable atom and emits some type of radiation. An atom's nucleus contains protons and neutrons. The protons have positive charges and repel each other, but the repulsive force between protons is only relevant over very small distances. The neutrons help separate the protons, enabling the strong nuclear force to hold the atom together. As the atomic number increases, this becomes more and more difficult. All atoms with atomic numbers greater than 83 are unstable. The three basic types of radioactive decay are alpha decay, beta decay, and gamma decay. The *half-life* is the length of time it takes for one-half of the atoms of a radioactive substance to decay into a new type of atom.

Fission reaction

A typical fission reaction is the fission of uranium-235 from neutron bombardment:

$${}^{235}_{92}\mathrm{U} + {}^{1}_{0}\mathrm{n} \rightarrow {}^{139}_{56}\mathrm{Ba} + {}^{94}_{36}\mathrm{Kr} + 3\,{}^{1}_{0}\mathrm{n}.$$

The uranium-235 atom (${}^{235}_{92}\mathrm{U}$) is bombarded by a neutron (${}^{1}_{0}\mathrm{n}$). This neutron is absorbed, forcing the uranium-235 atom into an excited, unstable state. This excited, unstable uranium-235 atom splits into smaller more stable pieces, which consist of a barium-139 atom (${}^{139}_{56}\mathrm{Ba}$), a krypton-94 atom (${}^{94}_{36}\mathrm{Kr}$), and three neutrons (${}^{1}_{0}\mathrm{n}$). These neutrons in turn may bombard other uranium-235 atoms causing the nuclear fission to continue.

Nuclear fusion

Nuclear fusion is the process in which the nuclei of light, unstable atoms unite or fuse to form a heavier, more stable atom. Fusion requires extremely high temperatures and often pressures that force the atoms into a plasma state. In this high-energy state, the atoms collide frequently and are able to fuse together. In this process, some mass is lost and released as large quantities of energy. The Sun's heat and light are produced by a fusion reaction in the Sun's core of four hydrogen atoms fusing into a helium nucleus.

Alpha emission

In alpha emission, the parent nuclide spits into two parts consisting of the daughter nuclide and an alpha particle. The alpha particle is identical to a helium nucleus and consists of two protons and two neutrons as represented by ${}^{4}_{2}\mathrm{He}$ or ${}^{4}_{2}\mathrm{He}^{2+}$. The daughter nuclide has a mass number that is four less than the parent nuclide and an atomic number that is two less than the parent nuclide. An example of alpha emission is the decay of an uranimum-238 atom into a thorium-234 atom and an alpha particle as shown below:

$${}^{238}_{92}\mathrm{U} \rightarrow {}^{234}_{90}\mathrm{Th} + {}^{4}_{2}\mathrm{He}.$$

Positive and negative beta decay

In positive beta decay, also known as positron emission, the parent nuclide splits into two parts consisting of the daughter nuclide and a positron. The positron is represented by ${}^{0}_{+1}\mathrm{e}$ because its mass is negligible compared to a neutron or proton, and its charge is + 1. The daughter nuclide has the same mass number as the parent nuclide and an atomic number of one less than the parent nuclide. An example of positive beta decay is when a carbon-11 atom splits into a boron-11 atom and a positron as given by the equation shown here:

$$^{11}_{6}C \rightarrow ^{11}_{5}B + ^{0}_{+1}e.$$

In negative beta decay, also simply called beta decay, the parent nuclide splits into two parts consisting of the daughter nuclide and an electron. The electron is represented by $^{0}_{-1}e$ because its mass is negligible compared to a neutron or proton, and its charge is −1. An example of negative beta decay is when a carbon-14 atom splits into a nitrogen-14 atom and an electron as given by the following equation:

$$^{14}_{6}C \rightarrow ^{14}_{7}N + ^{0}_{-1}e.$$

Electron capture

In electron capture, an electron from an atom's own electron cloud impacts the atom's nucleus and causes a decay reaction. The parent nuclide absorbs the electron, and a proton is converted to a neutron. A neutrino is emitted from the nucleus. Gamma radiation is also emitted. The daughter nuclide has the same mass number as the parent nuclide, and the atomic number of the daughter nuclide is one lower that the atomic number of the parent nuclide. An example of electron capture is when a nitrogen-13 atom absorbs an electron and converts to a carbon-13 atom while emitting a neutrino ($^{0}_{0}v$) and gamma radiation (γ) as shown by the following equation:

$$^{13}_{7}N + ^{0}_{-1}e \rightarrow ^{13}_{6}C + ^{0}_{0}v + \gamma.$$

Transmutation

Transmutation is a type of nuclear decay in which an atom is bombarded by high-speed particles to cause it to convert from one type of atom to another type of atom. Ernest Rutherford was the first to accomplish this with the transmutation of the nitrogen-14 atom into an oxygen-17 atom by bombardment with a beam of high-speed helium ions. In this transmutation, the helium-4 ion is also converted to a hydrogen-1 ion:

$$^{14}_{7}N + ^{4}_{2}He \rightarrow ^{17}_{8}O + ^{1}_{1}H.$$

Neutron radiation

Neutron radiation is a type of transmutation that is used to create many isotopes that do not occur naturally. In neutron radiation, an atom is bombarded by high-speed neutrons ($^{1}_{0}n$) to cause nuclear decay. In neutron radiation, the daughter nuclide has a mass number one higher than the parent nuclide but the atomic number remains the same. The daughter is an atom of the same element as the parent nuclide but has one more neutron, which makes it a different isotope of that element. An example of neutron radiation is when a cobalt-59 atom is bombarded by a high-speed neutron and converts to a cobalt-60 atom as shown in the following equation:

$$^{59}_{27}Co + ^{1}_{0}n \rightarrow ^{60}_{27}Co.$$

Balancing a nuclear reaction

When balancing a nuclear reaction, two key principles must be applied. First, the mass number must be conserved. Second, the atomic number must be conserved. To determine the products formed, the mass numbers and atomic numbers of the particles emitted or absorbed must be known. Alpha decay emits alpha particles ($^{4}_{2}He$). Beta decay emits electrons ($^{0}_{-1}e$). Positron decay emits positrons ($^{0}_{+1}e$). Neutron radiation absorbs neutrons ($^{1}_{0}n$). In alpha decay, the mass number decreases by four, and the atomic number decreases by two. In negative beta decay, the mass number stays the same and the atomic number increases by one. In positive beta decay, the mass number stays the same and the atomic number decreases by one. In neutron radiation, the mass number increases by one and the atomic number stays the same.

Balance the following nuclear reactions:

1. $^{230}_{90}Th \leftrightarrow {}^{4}_{2}He + \_\_\_\_.$
2. $^{40}_{19}K \leftrightarrow {}^{0}_{-1}e + \_\_\_\_.$

The key principles to completing or balancing nuclear reactions are that the mass number is conserved and the atomic number is conserved.

In number 1, thorium-230 under goes alpha decay and emits an alpha particle with a mass number of 4 and an atomic number of 2. Balancing the atomic numbers (90 – 2) yields an atomic number of 88, which corresponds to radium. Balancing the mass numbers (230 – 4) yields 226. Therefore, the missing product is $^{226}_{88}Ra$.

In number 2, potassium-40 undergoes beta decay and emits an electron with an assigned mass number of 0 and an assigned atomic number of –1. Balancing the atomic numbers (19 – (–1)) yields an atomic number of 20, which corresponds to calcium. Balancing the mass numbers (40 – 0) yields a mass number of 40. Therefore, the missing product is $^{40}_{20}Ca$.

Bonds

Chemical bonds are the attractive forces that bind atoms together into molecules. Atoms form chemical bonds in an attempt to satisfy the octet rule. These bond types include covalent bonds, ionic bonds, and metallic bonds. Covalent bonds are formed from the sharing of electron pairs between two atoms in a molecule. Ionic bonds are formed from the transferring of electrons between one atom and another, which results in the formations of cations and anions. Metallic bonding results from the sharing of delocalized electrons among all of the atoms in a molecule.

Polar covalent bonds result when electrons are shared unequally between atoms. Nonpolar covalent bonds result when electrons are shared equally between atoms. The unequal sharing of electrons is due to the differences in the electronegativities of the two atoms sharing the electrons. Partial charges develop due to this unequal sharing of electrons. The greater that the difference is in the electronegativities between the two atoms, the stronger the dipole is. For example, the covalent bonds formed between the carbon atom and the two oxygen atoms in carbon dioxide are polar covalent bonds because the electronegativities of carbon and oxygen differ slightly. If the electronegativities are equal, then the covalent bonds are nonpolar. For example, the covalent double bond between two oxygen atoms is nonpolar because the oxygen atoms have the same electronegativities.

Covalent bonds

Covalent bonding results from the sharing of electrons between atoms. Atoms seek to fill their valence shell and will share electrons with another atom in order to have a full octet (except hydrogen and helium, which only hold two electrons in their valence shells). Molecular compounds have covalent bonds. Organic compounds such as proteins, carbohydrates, lipids, and nucleic acids are molecular compounds formed by covalent bonds. Methane (CH_4) is a molecular compound in which one carbon atom is covalently bonded to four hydrogen atoms as shown below.

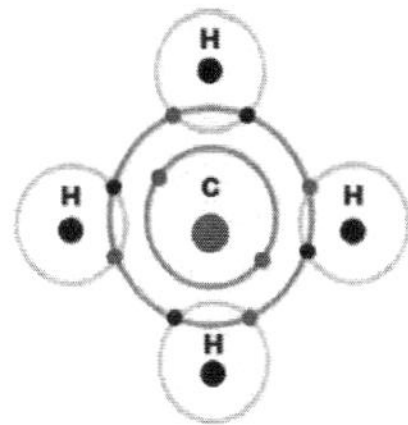

The bond length of a covalent bond is the distance between the nuclei of two covalently bonded atoms. The higher the bond order, the shorter the bond length. Single bonds are between one pair of electrons, and they are the weakest. Because single bonds (bond order 1) are the weakest, they are the longest of the three types of covalent bonds. Double bonds are between two pairs of electrons. Because double bonds (bond order 2) are stronger that single bonds, double bonds are shorter than single bonds. Triple bonds are between three pairs of electrons. Because triple bonds (bond order 3) are stronger than double bonds and single bonds, triple bonds have the shortest bond length.

The bond strength determines the amount of energy needed to break a covalent bond. Bond strength increases as bond length decreases. The bond length is the distance between the nuclei of two covalently bonded atoms. The higher the bond order, the shorter the bond length. Single bonds are between one pair of electrons, and they are the weakest. Double bonds are between two pairs of electrons. Double bonds (bond order 2) are stronger that single bonds. Triple bonds are between three pairs of electrons. Triple bonds (bond order 3) are stronger than double bonds and single bonds.

Ionic bonding

Ionic bonding results from the transfer of electrons between atoms. A cation or positive ion is formed when an atom loses one or more electrons. An anion or negative ion is formed when an atom gains one or more electrons. An ionic bond results from the electrostatic attraction between a cation and an anion. One example of a compound formed by ionic bonds is sodium chloride or NaCl. Sodium (Na) is an alkali metal and tends to form Na^+ ions. Chlorine is a halogen and tends to form Cl^- ions. The Na^+ ion and the Cl^- ion are attracted to each other. This electrostatic attraction between these oppositely charged ions is what results in the ionic bond between them.

$$Na\cdot + Cl \longrightarrow [Na]^+[Cl]^-$$

electron transer from sodium to chlorine

Metallic bonding

Metallic bonding is a type of bonding between metals. Metallic bonds are similar to covalent bonds in that they are a type of sharing of electrons between atoms. However, in covalent bonding, the electrons are shared with only one other atom. In metallic bonding, the electrons are shared with all the surrounding atoms. These electrons are referred to as delocalized electrons. Metallic bonding is responsible for many of the characteristics in metals including conductivity of heat and electricity, malleability, and ductility. An example of metallic bonding is the metallic bond between the copper atoms in a piece of copper wire.

Assigning atomic symbols to elements on the periodic table

The atomic symbol for many elements is simply the first letter of the element name. For example, the atomic symbol for hydrogen is H, and the atomic symbol for carbon is C. The atomic symbol of other elements is the first two letters of the element name. For example, the atomic symbol for helium is He, and the atomic symbol for cobalt is Co. The atomic symbols of several elements are derived from Latin. For example, the atomic symbol for copper (Cu) is derived from *cuprum,* and the atomic symbol for iron (Fe) is derived from *ferrum.* The atomic symbol for tungsten (W) is derived from the German word *wolfram.*

Groups and periods

A group is a vertical column of the periodic table. Elements in the same group have the same number of valence electrons. For the representative elements, the number of valence electrons is equal to the group number. Because of their equal valence electrons, elements in the same groups have similar physical and chemical properties. A period is a horizontal row of the periodic table. Atomic number increases from left to right across a row. The period of an element corresponds to the highest energy level of the electrons in the atoms of that element. The energy level increases from top to bottom down a group.

Atomic number and atomic mass

The elements in the periodic table are arranged in order of increasing atomic number first left to right and then top to bottom across the periodic table. The atomic number represents the number of protons in the atoms of that element. Because of the increasing numbers of protons, the atomic mass typically also increases from left to right across a period and from top to bottom down a row. The atomic mass is a weighted average of all the naturally occurring isotopes of an element.

Arrangement of the transition elements

The transition elements belong to one of two categories consisting of the transition metals and the inner transition metals. The transition metals are located in the middle of the periodic table, and the inner transition metals are typically set off as two rows by themselves at the bottom of the periodic table. The transition metals correspond to the "*d* block" for orbital filling, and the inner transition metals correspond to the "*f* block" for orbital filling. Examples of transition metals include iron, copper, nickel, and zinc. The inner transition metals consist of the *lanthanide* or *rare-earth series,* which corresponds to the first row, and the *actinide series,* which corresponds to the second row of the inner transition metals. The *lanthanide series* includes lanthanum, cerium, and praseodymium. The *actinide series* includes actinium, uranium, and plutonium.

Arrangement of metals, nonmetals, and metalloids

The metals are located on the left side and center of the periodic table, and the nonmetals are located on the right side of the periodic table. The metalloids or semimetals form a zigzag line between the metals and nonmetals as shown below. Metals include the alkali metals such as lithium, sodium, and potassium and the alkaline earth metals such as beryllium, magnesium, and calcium. Metals also include the transition metals such as iron, copper, and nickel and the inner transition metals such as thorium, uranium, and plutonium. Nonmetals include the chalcogens such as oxygen and sulfur, the halogens such as fluorine and chlorine, and the noble gases such as helium and argon. Carbon, nitrogen, and phosphorus are also nonmetals. Metalloids or semimetals include boron, silicon, germanium, antimony, and polonium.

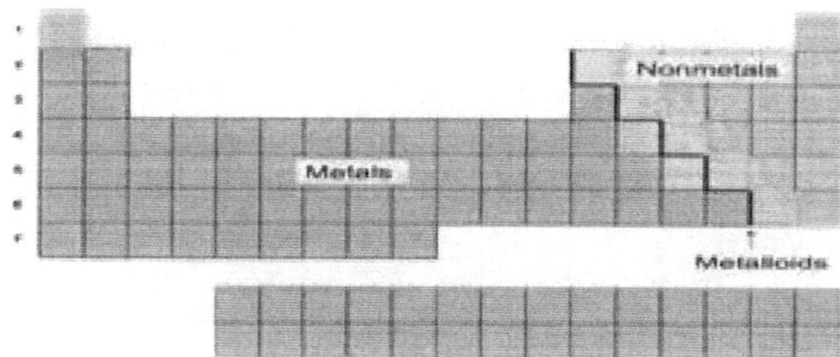

Atomic radius size

Atomic radius size decreases across a period from left to right and increases down a group from top to bottom. The atomic radius decreases across a period due to the increasing number of protons and the attraction between those protons and the orbiting electrons. The atomic radius increases down a group due to the increasing energy levels. Atoms in the top-right corner of the periodic table (including hydrogen) have the smallest atomic radii, and atoms in the bottom-left corner of the periodic table have the largest atomic radii. Helium has the smallest atomic radius, and francium has the largest atomic radius.

Ionic radius size

The ionic radius size increases down a group of the periodic table. This is due to the increasing energy levels and the fact that electrons are orbiting farther and farther from the nucleus. The trend seen across the periods of the periodic table is due to the formation of cations or anions. Metals form cations or positive ions. Cations are smaller than their neutral atoms due to the loss of one or more electrons. Nonmetals except the noble gases form anions or negative ions. Anions are larger than their neutral atoms due to the gain of one or more electrons.

Ionization energy

Ionization energy is the amount of energy needed to remove an electron from an isolated atom. Ionization energy decreases down a group of the periodic table because the electrons get farther and farther from the nucleus making it easier for the electron to be removed. Ionization energy increases across a period of the periodic table due to the decreasing atomic size, which is due to the increasing number of protons attracting the electrons towards the nucleus. These trends of ionization energy are the opposite of the trends for atomic radius.

Electron affinity

Electron affinity is the energy required to add an electron to a neutral atom in the gaseous phase of an element. Electron affinity values typically range from less negative to more negative. If electrons are added to a halogen such as fluorine or chlorine, energy is released and the electron affinity is negative. If electrons are added to an alkaline earth metal, energy is absorbed and the electron affinity is positive. In general, electron affinity becomes more negative from left to right across a period in the periodic table. Electron affinity becomes less negative from the top to the bottom of a group of the periodic table.

Electronegativity

Electronegativity is a measure of the ability of an atom that is chemically combined to at least one other atom in a molecule to attract electrons to it. The Pauling scale is commonly used to assign values to the elements, with fluorine, which is the most electronegative element, being assigned a value of 4.0. Electronegativity increases from left to right across a period of the periodic table and decreases from top to bottom down a group of the periodic table.

Physical properties of the elements

The boiling point, melting point, and conductivity of the elements depend partially on the number of valence electrons of the atoms of those elements. For the representative elements in groups 1A–8A, the number of valence electrons matches the group number. Because all of the elements in each individual group contain the same number of valence electrons, elements in the same groups tend to have similar boiling points, melting points, and conductivity. Boiling points and melting points tend to decrease moving down the column of groups 1A–4A and 8A but increase slightly moving down the column of groups 5A–7A.

Chemical reactivity of the elements

Atoms of elements in the same group or family of the periodic table tend to have similar chemical properties and similar chemical reactions. For example, the alkali metals, which form cations with a charge of 1+, tend to react with water to form hydrogen gas and metal hydroxides. The alkaline earth metals, which form cations with a charge of 2+, react with oxygen gas to form metal oxides. The halogens, which form anions with a charge of 1–, are highly reactive and toxic. The noble gases are unreactive and never form compounds naturally.

Chemical Reactions and Properties of Matter

Process for naming binary ionic compounds

The names of binary ionic compounds follow this pattern:

- cation name (space) anion name.

The name of simple cations is usually the element name. For example, the K^+ cation is named potassium. Some cations exist in more than one form. In those cases, the charge of the ion follows the element as a Roman numeral in parentheses. For example, the Cu^+ ion is named copper(I) and the Cu^{2+} ion is named copper(II). Simple anions are named with the root of the element name followed by the suffix *-ide.* For example, the O^{2-} anion is named oxide, and the F^- ion is named fluoride. The following are some examples of names of binary ionic compounds: KI is named potassium iodide, and FeO is named iron(II) oxide.

<u>Examples</u>

N_2O_4 — This is a binary molecular compound. Using the prefixes *di-* for 2 and *tetra-* for 4, this compound is named dinitrogen tetroxide. Note that the entire element name is retained for the cation, but the root plus *-ide* is used for the anion name.

S_2F_{10} — This is a binary molecular compound. Using the prefixes *di-* for 2 and *deca-* for 10, this compound is named disulfur decafluoride. Note that the entire element name is retained for the cation, but the root plus *-ide* is used for the anion name.

Fe_2O_3 — This is a binary ionic compound. Iron forms two types of cations Fe^{2+} and Fe^{3+}, but because the anion is O^{2-}, this must be the Fe^{3+} ion in order to balance the charges. This compound is named iron(III) oxide.

$CuCl_2$ — This is a binary ionic compound. Copper forms two types of cations Cu^+ and Cu^{2+}, but because the anion is Cl^-, this must be the Cu^{2+} ion in order to balance the charges. This compound is named copper(II) chloride.

Binary molecular compounds

The names of binary molecular compounds follow this pattern:
prefix + first element name (space) prefix + root of second element name + -ide.

If a prefix ends with *a* or *o* and the element name begins with *a* or *o*, the first *a* or *o* of the prefix is dropped. For example, N_2O_5 is named dinitrogen pentoxide. The prefix *mono-* is usually dropped unless more than one binary compound may be formed from the two elements involved.

Binary Molecular Compounds			
#	Prefix	#	Prefix
1	mono-	6	hexa-
2	di-	7	hepta-
3	tri-	8	octa-
4	tetra-	9	nona-
5	penta-	10	deca-

Naming acids

Acids are generally categorized as binary acids or oxyacids. Binary acids are named by the pattern: *hydro-* + root of element + *-ic* (space) acid. For example, HI is named hydroiodic acid, and HCl is named hydrochloric acid. One exception is that in hydrosulfuric acid (H_2S), the entire element name sulfur is used. The names of oxyacids depend on the endings of their polyatomic anions. If the polyatomic anions end in *-ate*, then the acid names end in *-ic*. If the anions end in *-ite*, the acid names end in *-ous*. The naming pattern for an oxyacid is as follows: anion root + ending (space) acid. For example, H_2CO_3 is named carbonic acid because the carbonate ion ends in *-ate*, and H_2SO_3 is named sulfurous acid because the sulfite ion ends in *-ite.*

Naming bases and salts

Bases typically are ionic compounds with the hydroxide anion and are named following the conventions of naming ionic compounds. For example, NaOH is named sodium hydroxide and $Mg(OH)_2$ is named magnesium hydroxide. Salts are ionic compounds with any cation except H^+ from an aqueous base and any anion except OH^- from an aqueous acid. Salts are named like regular ionic compounds with the name of the cation followed by the name of the anion. Examples of salts include sodium chloride (NaCl), potassium fluoride (KF), magnesium iodide (MgI_2), $NaC_2H_5O_2$ (sodium acetate), and ammonium carbonate ($(NH_4)_2CO_3$).

Hydrates

Hydrates form from salts (ionic compounds) that attract water. Hydrates are named from their salt (ionic compound) name and the number of water molecules involved in the following pattern: salt name (space) prefix + hydrate.

For example, the name of $CuSO_4 \cdot 5H_2O$ is copper(II) sulfate pentahydrate, and the name of $CoCl_2 \cdot 6H_2O$ is cobalt(II) chloride hexahydrate.

Binary Molecular Compounds			
#	Prefix	#	Prefix
1	mono-	6	hexa-
2	di-	7	hepta-
3	tri-	8	octa-
4	tetra-	9	nona-
5	penta-	10	deca-

Balancing a chemical equation

According to the law of conservation of mass, the mass of the products must always equal the mass of the reactants in a chemical reaction. Because mass is conserved, the number of each type of atom in the products must equal the number of each type of atom in the reactants. The key to balancing a chemical reaction is in balancing the number of each type of atom on both sides of the equation. Only the coefficients in front of the reactants and products may be changed to accomplish this, not the subscripts in the molecules themselves. Try balancing the largest number of a type of atom first. Also, check if any odd numbers need to be changed to even. Always leave the uncombined elements to balance until the end.

Example #1

Balance the equation $KNO_3(s) \rightarrow KNO_2(s) + O_2(g)$.

First, determine the types and numbers of each type of atom on each side of the equation:

Reactants		Products	
K	1	K	1
N	1	N	1
O	3	O	4

"Oxygen" needs to be balanced. Add a coefficient of "2" to the left side to force "oxygen" to be even and update the counts:

Reactants		Products	
K	2	K	1
N	2	N	1
O	6	O	4

Now, balance the potassium and nitrogen by placing a coefficient of "2" in front of the KNO_2 and update the counts:

Reactants		Products	
K	2	K	2
N	2	N	2
O	6	O	6

The equation is now balanced: $2KNO_3(s) \rightarrow 2KNO_2(s) + O_2(g)$.

Example #2

Balance the equation $C_2H_2(g) + O_2(g) \rightarrow CO_2(g) + H_2O(g)$.

First, determine the types and numbers of each type of atom on each side of the equation:

Reactants		Products	
C	2	C	1
H	2	H	2
O	2	O	3

"Oxygen" needs to be balanced, but remember to leave the uncombined oxygen reactant until the end. "Carbon" also needs to be balanced. Add a coefficient of "4" to the CO_2 on the right side and a coefficient of "2" in front of the C_2H_2 and update the counts:

Reactants		Products	
C	4	C	4
H	4	H	2
O	2	O	9

Balance the "hydrogen" by adding a "2" in front of the H_2O and update the counts:

Reactants		Products	
C	4	C	4
H	4	H	4
O	2	O	10

Finally, balance the "oxygen" by adding a "5" in front of the O_2 on the left.

The equation is now balanced: $2C_2H_2$ (g) + $5O_2$ (g) → $4CO_2$ (g) + $2H_2O$ (g).

Balanced chemical equation involving a simple oxidation-reduction reaction

One method to balance simple oxidation-reduction reactions is to split the reaction into half-reactions. First, write the oxidation half-reaction and the reduction half-reaction. Remember the phrase *"LEO the lion says GER,"* which is a reminder that the loss of electrons is oxidation, and the gain of electrons is reduction. Next, balance the electrons by multiply the equation(s) by the necessary factor(s). Finally, cancel the electron(s) and combine the balanced oxidation and reduction half-reactions into a balanced net chemical equation.

Examples

$Na + O_2 \rightarrow Na^+ + O^{2-}$
In order to balance the equation $Na + O_2 \rightarrow Na^+ + O^{2-}$, first, write the individual half-reactions:
oxidation: $Na \rightarrow Na^+ + e^-$
reduction: $O_2 + 4e^- \rightarrow 2O^{2-}$.

Next, balance the number of electrons by multiplying the oxidation half-reaction by 4:
oxidation: $4Na \rightarrow 4Na^+ + 4e^-$
reduction: $O_2 + 4e^- \rightarrow 2O^{2-}$.

Finally, cancel the electrons and combine the half-reactions into the net reaction:
$4Na + O_2 \rightarrow 4Na^+ + 2O^{2-}$.

Balanced equation examples

Write a balanced equation for the combustion of methane.

The molecular formula for methane is CH_4. For a combustion equation, the reactants are methane (CH_4) and oxygen gas (O_2). The products of this combustion reaction are water vapor (H_2O) and carbon dioxide (CO_2). Setting up the equation yields the following reaction:
CH_4 (g) + O_2 (g) → CO_2 (g) + H_2O (g).
This equation must still be balanced. Finally, the combustion of methane is given by the following reaction:
CH_4 (g) + $2O_2$ (g) → CO_2 (g) + $2H_2O$ (g).

Explain how to write a balanced equation for the neutralization of hydrochloric acid, HCl (aq), with sodium hydroxide, NaOH (aq).

In a neutralization reaction, an acid reacts with a base to form a salt and water. The salt forms from the cation of the base and the anion of the acid. The salt formed from these reactants is NaCl with the Na^+ from the base and the Cl^- from the acid. Water forms from the remaining H^+ and OH^- ions:
acid + base → salt + water
HCl (aq) + NaOH (aq) → NaCl (aq) + H_2O (l).

Write a balanced equation for the decomposition reaction of solid lithium carbonate (Li_2CO_3).

The general form for a decomposition reaction is AB → A + B. However, this metal oxide has three elements and may at first not seem to fit the general form. When many metal carbonates are heated, they form the metal oxide and carbon dioxide gas. In this case, the products will also be compounds. In this decomposition reaction, when heated, solid lithium oxide decomposes to form solid lithium oxide and gaseous carbon dioxide:
$Li_2CO_3(s) \xrightarrow{\Delta} LiO(s) + CO_2(g)$.

Write a balanced equation for the dehydration of ethanol.

Ethanol (C_2H_5OH) can be dehydrated to produce ethane (C_2H_4). The gaseous ethanol is passed over a hot aluminum oxide catalyst to produce ethane and water.
$\text{ethanol} \xrightarrow{\text{aluminum oxide}} \text{ethane + water}$
$C_2H_5OH\ (g) \xrightarrow{Al_2O_3} C_2H_4\ (g) + H_2O\ (l)$.
This can also be shown in the form of condensed structural formulas:
$CH_3CH_2OH \xrightarrow{Al_2O_3} CH_2 = CH_2 + H_2O$.

Describe the general forms for single- and double-replacement reactions. Give an example of each.

Single-replacement reactions, which are also known as single-displacement reactions or substitution reactions, have the general form of A + BC → AC + B. An example of a single-replacement reaction is the displacement of hydrogen from hydrochloric acid by zinc metal as given in the following equation:
Zn (s) + 2HCl (aq) → $ZnCl_2$ (aq) + H_2 (aq).

Double-replacement reactions, which are also known as double-displacement reactions, have the general form of AB + CD → AD + CB. An example of a double-replacement reaction is when aqueous solutions of lead(II) nitrate and potassium iodide react to form solid lead(II) iodide and aqueous potassium nitrate as given by the following equation:
$Pb(NO_3)_2$ (aq) + 2KI (aq) → PbI_2 (s) + $2KNO_3$ (aq).

Explain how to identify each reaction type as a single- or double-replacement reaction, and predict the products of Mg (s) + 2 H_2O (l) →.

This reaction must be a single-replacement reaction because the left side corresponds to the left side of the general equation A + BC → AB + C. In this case, the magnesium replaces some of the hydrogen, and the products are hydrogen gas and magnesium hydroxide.
Mg (s) + $2H_2O$ (l) → $Mg(OH)_2$ (aq) + H_2 (g).

Explain how to identify each reaction type as a single- or double-replacement reaction, and predict the products of $Pb(NO_3)_2$ (aq) + 2 KI (aq) →.

2. This reaction must be a double-replacement reaction because the left side corresponds to the left side of the general equation AB + CD → AD + CB. In this case, the Pb^+ cation from the $Pb(NO_3)_2$ bonds with the I^- anion from the KI to form solid PbI_2. The NO_3^- anion from the $Pb(NO_3)_2$ bonds with the K^+ cation from the KI to form aqueous KNO_3. $Pb(NO_3)_2$ (aq) + 2KI (aq) → PbI_2 (s) + $2KNO_3$ (aq).

Write a balanced equation for the oxidation-reduction reaction of metallic zinc powder and aqueous copper(II) sulfate.

According to the activity series, zinc is more reactive than copper. Therefore, the zinc is oxidized, and the copper is reduced. Write the half-reactions:
oxidation: Zn → Zn^{2+} + $2e^-$.

reduction: Cu^{2+} + $2e^-$ → Cu.

Cancel the electrons and combine the two half-reactions into the net equation:
Zn + Cu^{2+} → Zn^{2+} + Cu.

Finally, add the symbols to indicate the state of each reactant and product:
Zn (s) + Cu^{2+} (aq) → Zn^{2+} (aq) + Cu (s).

Interestingly, this equation can also be written as the following single-displacement reaction:
Zn (s) + $CuSO_4$ (aq) → $ZnSO_4$ (aq) + Cu (s).

This single-displacement reaction has the same net ionic equation after canceling out the spectator ions.

Write a balanced equation for the oxidation-reduction reaction of a piece of solid copper wire immersed in an aqueous solution of silver nitrate.

According to the activity series, copper is more reactive than silver. Therefore, the copper is oxidized, and the silver is reduced. Write the half-reactions:
oxidation: $Cu \rightarrow Cu^{2+} + 2e^{-}$.

reduction: $Ag^{+} + e^{-} \rightarrow Ag$.

Multiply the reduction half-reaction by 2 to balance the number of electrons:
oxidation: $Cu \rightarrow Cu^{2+} + 2e^{-}$.

reduction: $2Ag^{+} + 2e^{-} \rightarrow 2Ag$.

Cancel the electrons and combine the two half-reactions into the net equation:
$Cu + 2Ag^{+} \rightarrow Cu^{2+} + 2Ag$.

Finally, add the symbols to indicate the state of each reactant and product:
$Cu\ (s) + 2Ag^{+}\ (aq) \rightarrow Cu^{2+}\ (aq) + 2Ag\ (s)$.

Note that this equation is also classified as a single-displacement reaction:
$Cu\ (s) + 2AgNO_3\ (aq) \rightarrow Cu(NO_3)_2\ (aq) + 2Ag\ (s)$.

This single-displacement reaction has the same net ionic equation after canceling out the spectator ions.

Dilute and concentrated

The terms *dilute* and *concentrated* have opposite meanings. In a solution, the solute is dissolved in the solvent. The more solvent that is dissolved, the more concentrated is the solution. The less solute that is dissolved, the less concentrated and the more dilute is the solution. The terms are often associated with the preparation of a stock solution for a laboratory experiment. Stock solutions are typically ordered in a concentrated solution. To prepare for use in a chemistry lab, the stock solutions are diluted to the appropriate molarity by adding a specific amount of solvent such as water to a specific amount of stock solution.

Saturated, unsaturated, and supersaturated

The terms *saturated, unsaturated,* and *supersaturated* are associated with solutions. In a solution, a solvent is added to a solvent. In a saturated solution, the solute is added to the solvent until no more solute is able to dissolve. The undissolved solute will settle down to the bottom of the beaker. A solution is considered unsaturated as long as more solute is able to go into solution under ordinary conditions. The solubility of solids in liquids typically increases as temperature increases. If the temperature of a solution is increased as the solute is being added, more solute than is normally possible may go into solution, forming a supersaturated solution.

Solvent and solute

A solution is a homogeneous mixture that consists of a solute and a solvent. In general terms, the solute is the substance that is being dissolved and the solvent is the substance doing the dissolving. Ionic compounds dissociate, and molecular compounds ionize in solution. Typically, the solute is the substance that is present in the greater amount and the solvent is the substance that is present in the lesser amount. For example, in a glucose solution, the glucose would be considered the solute, and the water would be considered the solvent.

Calculating the molarity and molality of a solution

Molarity and molality are measures of the concentration of a solution. Molarity (M) is the amount of solute in moles per the amount of solution in liters. A 1.0 M solution consists of 1.0 mole of solute for each 1.0 L of solution. Molality (m) is the amount of solute in moles per the amount of solvent in kilograms. A 1.0 m solution consists of 1.0 mole of solute for each 1.0 kg of solvent. Often, when performing these calculations, the amount of solute is given in grams. To convert from grams of solute to moles of solute, multiply the grams of solute by the molar mass of the solute:

- Molarity (M) = $\frac{\text{moles of solute (mol)}}{\text{liters of solution (L)}}$. Molality (m) = $\frac{\text{moles of solute (mol)}}{\text{kilograms of solvent (kg)}}$.

Calculating mole fraction, parts per million, parts per billion, and percent by mass or volume

Concentrations can be measured in mole fractions, parts per million, parts per billion, and percent by mass or volume. Mole fraction (χ) is calculated by dividing the number of moles of one component by the total number of moles of all of the components of the solution. Parts per million (ppm) is calculated by dividing the mass of the solute in grams by the mass of the solvent and solute in grams and then multiplying the quotient by 1,000,000 ppm. Parts per billion (ppb) is calculated similarly, except the quotient is multiplied by 1,000,000,000 ppb. Percent concentration can be calculated by mass or by volume by dividing the mass or volume of the solute by the mass or volume of the solution. This quotient is a decimal that can be converted to a percent by multiplying by 100.

Calculate the molarity of 100.0 g of $CaCl_2$ in 500.0 mL of solution.

To calculate molarity, use the formula molarity (M) = $\frac{\text{moles of solute (mol)}}{\text{liters of solution (L)}}$. The necessary conversions from grams $CaCl_2$ to moles $CaCl_2$ and from 500.0 mL to liters may be performed using dimensional analysis. An alternate method of working this problem would be doing the conversions first and then substituting those values directly into the equation. Using the method of dimensional analysis and substituting the given information into the equation yields molarity = $\frac{100.0 \text{ grams CaCl}_2}{500.0 \text{ mL of solution}}$. Adding the necessary conversions using dimensional analysis yields

$$\text{molarity} = \left(\frac{100.0 \text{ g CaCl}_2}{500.0 \text{ mL of solution}}\right)\left(\frac{\text{mol CaCl}_2}{110.98 \text{ g}}\right)\left(\frac{1000 \text{ mL}}{\text{L}}\right) = 1.802 \text{ M}.$$

Preparing a dilute solution from a stock solution

In order to prepare a dilute solution from a stock solution, the molarity and the needed volume of the diluted solution as well as the molarity of the stock solution must be known. The volume of the stock solution to be diluted can be calculated using the formula $V_{stock}M_{stock} = V_{dilute}M_{dilute}$, where V_{stock} is the unknown variable, M_{stock} is the molarity of the stock solution, V_{dilute} is the needed volume of the dilute solution, and M_{dilute} is the needed molarity of the dilute solution. Solving this formula for V_{stock} yields $V_{stock} = \frac{V_{dilute}M_{dilute}}{M_{stock}}$. Then, dilute the calculated amount of stock solution (V_{stock}) to the total volume required of the diluted solution.

Effects of temperature, pressure, surface area, and agitation on the dissolution rate

Temperature, pressure, surface area, and agitation affect the dissolution rate. Increasing the temperature increases the kinetic energy of the molecules, which increases the number of collisions with the solute particles. Increasing the surface area of contact by stirring (agitation) or crushing a solid solute also increases the dissolution rate and helps prevent recrystallization. Increasing the pressure will increase the dissolution rate for gas solutes in liquid solvents because the added pressure will make it more difficult for the gas to escape. Increasing the pressure will have virtually no effect on the dissolution rate for solid solutes in liquid solvents under normal conditions.

Effect of temperature and pressure on solubility

Temperature and pressure affect solubility. For gas solutes in liquid solvents, increasing the temperature increases the kinetic energy causing more gas particles to escape the surface of the liquid solvents and therefore decreasing the solubility of the solutes. For most solid solutes in liquid solvents, increasing the temperature increases the solubility, as shown in this solubility curve for selected salts. For gas solutes in liquid solvents, increasing the pressure increases the solubility. Increasing the pressure of liquid or solid solutes in liquid solvents has virtually no effect under normal conditions.

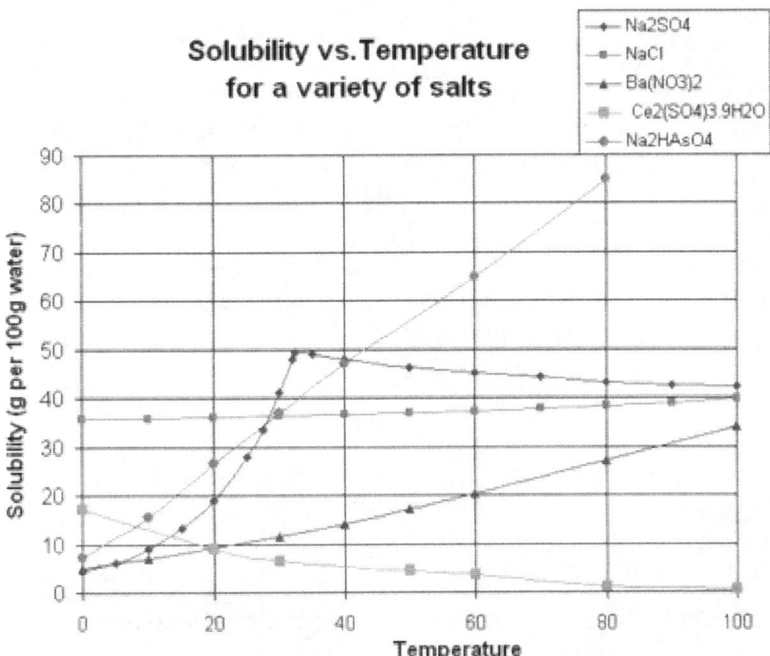

Acids and bases

Several differences exist between acids and bases. Acidic solutions tend to taste sour, whereas basic solutions tend to taste bitter. Dilute bases tend to feel slippery, whereas dilute acids feel like water. Active metals such as magnesium and zinc react with acids to produce hydrogen gas, but active metals usually do not react with bases. Acids and bases form electrolytes in aqueous solutions and conduct electricity. Acids turn blue litmus red, but bases turn red litmus blue. Acidic solutions have a pH of less than 7, whereas basic solutions have a pH of greater than 7.

Arrhenius acid and base

Arrhenius acids are substances that produce hydrogen ions (H^+) when dissolved in water to form aqueous solutions. Arrhenius bases are substances that produce hydroxide ions (OH^-) when dissolved in water to form aqueous solutions. The Arrhenius concept is limited to acids and bases in aqueous solutions and cannot be applied to other solids, liquids, and gases. Examples of Arrhenius acids include hydrochloric acid (HCl) and sulfuric acid (H_2SO_4). Examples of Arrhenius bases include sodium hydroxide (NaOH) and magnesium hydroxide ($Mg(OH)_2$).

Brønsted–Lowry acid and base

The Brønsted–Lowry concept is based on the donation or the acceptance of a proton. According to the Brønsted–Lowry concept, an acid is a substance that donates one or more protons to another substance and a base is a substance that accepts a proton from another substance. The Brønsted–Lowry concept can be applied to substances other than aqueous solutions. This concept is much broader than the Arrhenius concept, which can only be applied to aqueous solutions. The Brønsted–Lowry concept states that a substance cannot act like an acid (donate its proton) unless another substance is available to act as a base (accept the donated proton). In this concept, water may act as either an acid or a base. Hydrochloric acid (HCl) is an example of a Brønsted–Lowry acid. Ammonia (NH_3) is an example of a Brønsted–Lowry base.

Lewis acid and base

A Lewis acid is any substance that can accept a pair of nonbonding electrons. A Lewis base is any substance that can donate a pair of nonbonding electrons. According to the Lewis theory, all cations such as Mg^{2+} and Cu^{2+} are Lewis acids. Trigonal planar molecules, which are exceptions to the octet rule such as BF_3, are Lewis acids. Molecules such as CO_2 that have multiple bonds between two atoms that differ in electronegativities are Lewis acids, also. According to the Lewis theory, all anions such as OH^- are Lewis bases. Other examples of Lewis bases include trigonal pyramidal molecules such as ammonia, NH_3, and nonmetal oxides such as carbon dioxide, CO_2. Some compounds such as water, H_2O, can be either Lewis acids or bases.

Neutralization reaction

Neutralization is a reaction of an acid and a base that yields a salt and water. The salt is formed from the cation of the base and the anion of the acid. The water is formed from the cation of the acid and the anion of the base: acid + base → salt + water

An example is the neutralization reaction of hydrochloric acid and sodium hydroxide to form sodium chloride and water:

- HCl (aq) + NaOH (aq) → NaCl (s) + H_2O (l).

Equivalence point

The *equivalence point* is by definition the point in a titration at which the analyte is neutralized. When the acid–base indicator starts to change color, the equivalence point has been reached. At this point, equivalent amounts of acids and bases have reacted. Also, at this point, $[H^+] = [OH^-]$. On an acid–base titration curve, the slope of the curve increases dramatically at the equivalence point. For strong acids and bases, the equivalence point occurs at a pH of 7. The figures below show the equivalence points for a strong acid titrated with a strong base (a) and a strong base titrated with a strong acid (b).

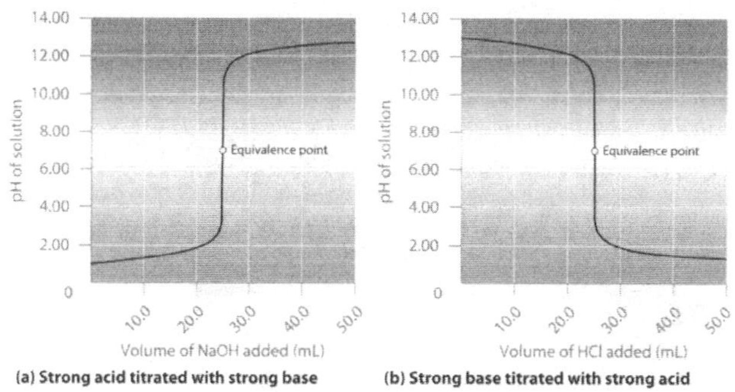

(a) Strong acid titrated with strong base (b) Strong base titrated with strong acid

pH scale

The pH scale categorizes the acidity or alkalinity (basicity) of a solution. The pH value may be calculated by the formula $pH = -\log[H^+]$, where $[H^+]$ is the concentration of hydrogen ions. The pH scales ranges from 0 to 14 with pH values near zero indicating the strongest acids and pH values near 14 indicating the strongest bases. With the pH scale, any solution with a $pH < 7$ is considered an acid and any solution with a $pH > 7$ is considered a base. Solutions with a pH of 7 are considered to be neutral.

Relationship between pH and pOH

The pH of a solution may be calculated using the formula $pH = -\log[H^+]$, where $[H^+]$ is the concentration of hydrogen ions. The pOH of a solution may be calculated using the formula $pOH = -\log[OH^-]$, where $[OH^-]$ is the concentration of hydroxide ions. The sum of the pH of a solution and the pOH of a solution is always 14. The pH of this HCl solution may be calculated using the formula $pH = -\log[0.0010\ M] = 3$. The sum of the pH and pOH is always 14. Therefore, the pOH may be calculated by the formula $14 - 3 = 11$.

Example

> *Calculate $[H^+]$ and $[OH^-]$ when given the pH or pOH. Given a solution with a pOH of 8.2, explain how to calculate pH, $[H^+]$, and $[OH^-]$.*
>
> Because $pH = -\log[H^+]$, the $[H^+]$ may be calculated by $[H^+] = \text{antilog}(-pH)$. Because $pOH = -\log[OH^-]$, the $[OH^-]$ may be calculated by $[OH^-] = \text{antilog}(-pOH)$. Also, because the $pH + pOH = 14$, the pOH may be calculated by the formula $14 - pH = pOH$. For example, given a solution with a pOH pf 8.0, the $[OH^-] = \text{antilog}(-8.0) = 1.0 \times 10^{-8}$. The $pH = 14 - 8.0 = 6.0$. The $[H^+] = \text{antilog}(-6.0) = 1 \times 10^{-6}$.

K_w

Pure water dissociates to a very small extent and reaches this equilibrium: $H_2O(l) + H_2O(l) \leftrightarrow H_3O^+ (aq) + OH^- (aq)$. The equilibrium constant for this equilibrium is called the ion product constant of water, or K_w. The constant K_w can be represented by $K_w = [H_3O^+][OH^-]$. The reactant H_2O is not represented in the equilibrium expression because it is essentially a pure liquid. The ion product constant of water K_w varies with temperature. As temperature increases, K_w increases and pH decreases. Therefore, this constant must be given at a specific temperature. At 25 °C, $[H_3O^+] = [OH^-] = 1 \times 10^{-7}$ M, which corresponds to pure water being neutral with a pH of 7.

Energy, Force, and Motion

Heat and temperature

Heat, or thermal energy, is a measure of the kinetic energy of the atoms within a substance. Heat, being a form of energy, has SI units of joules, but is also commonly measured in calories. The amount of heat a substance contains is generally quantified as a temperature. Temperature has SI units of degrees Celsius, though degrees Fahrenheit are also widely used.

It is often useful to know how much heat is required to cause a certain amount of material to reach a desired temperature. Each material has a property called specific heat, which allows this calculation. To bring about a temperature increase ΔT to a mass m made of a material with specific heat C, the required heat input is found by the equation $Q = mC\Delta T$. This equation can also be used to calculate the amount of heat absorbed during a given temperature increase. The amount of heat required to raise the temperature of a gram of water by one degree Celcius, or one Kelvin, is one calorie, or 4.184 J. Thus, the specific heat of water is 1 cal/g-K.

Temperature scales

Each of the temperature scales, Celsius and Fahrenheit, has a corresponding absolute temperature scale, Kelvin and Rankine, respectively. A temperature of zero Kelvin or zero Rankine is known as absolute zero, at which point there is theoretically no atomic motion or thermal energy. Kelvins and degrees Celsius are related by the equation, $T\ °C = (T + 273.15)\ K$. Similarly, Rankines and degrees Fahrenheit are related as $T\ °F = (T + 459.67)\ R$. From these relations, we can see that within both individual pairs of temperature scales, the magnitude of the unit is the same; that is, an increase of 1 °C is the same an increase of 1 K, while an increase of 1 °F equals an increase of 1 R. Converting from Fahrenheit to Celsius is slightly more complicated: $T\ °F = (5/9)(T - 32)\ °C$, or in reverse, $T\ °C = ((9/5)T + 32)\ °F$. From these equations, we can see that a degree Celsius is greater than a degree Fahrenheit.

Thermal expansion

When heated, most materials will undergo some amount of expansion. Though this is generally quite small, it is important to know how much of an impact this thermal expansion might have on the size of the object in question. Each material has a linear coefficient of thermal expansion α, generally having units of 1/°C or 1/°F, that relates the additional length to the original length. The percentage change in length is found by the equation $\Delta L/L_0 = \alpha\Delta T$, or to find the absolute change, $\Delta L = L_0\alpha\Delta T$. Just as heating the material causes it to expand, cooling it will cause it to contract.

Assuming that the material is able to expand in all directions, there will similarly be a change in areas and volumes. The change in an area A_0 will be $\Delta A = 2\alpha A_0\Delta T + \alpha^2\Delta T^2$. Because α is generally much less than 1, $\alpha^2\Delta T^2$ will most often be negligible. Thus the change in area becomes $\Delta A = 2\alpha A_0\Delta T$. From this we can see that the area coefficient of thermal expansion is $\gamma = 2\alpha$, and $\Delta A = \gamma A_0\Delta T$. By making similar assumptions with the equation for change in volume, we find that the volume coefficient of thermal expansion is $\beta = 3\alpha$ and that $\Delta V = \beta V_0\Delta T$.

Latent heat and specific heat

Suppose we wish to convert ice initially at -5 °C to water at 5 °C. We must provide heat to accomplish this. The amount of heat required to raise the temperature of a given quantity of a material is a property known as specific heat. This is most often given on a mass basis, with units of J/g-K, but may also be given as a molar property as J/mol-K. If the given quantity of material and the given specific heat are not unit compatible, it will be necessary to multiply or divide by the molar weight of the material to achieve compatibility. Returning to the problem at hand, in order for ice initially at -5 °C to reach 5 °C, it must undergo a phase change, from a solid to a liquid. When the ice is heated, it does not simply become water when it reaches 0 °C. In order for the ice to become water, additional heat must be added to break the bonds of the solid. This heat is called the latent heat of fusion and, like the specific heat, may be given on a mass or a molar basis, with common units of kJ/g or kJ/mol, respectively. This heat input for the phase change occurs while the material remains at a constant temperature. Once the phase change has been completed, the water temperature will begin to rise again with heat input, though the specific heat of liquid water will be different from that of ice. If the water need be heated above 100 °C, it will have to undergo a second phase change, overcoming the latent heat of vaporization, and its temperature will subsequently be governed by a third specific heat, that of the gas phase.

Conduction

Heat always flows from a region of higher temperature to a region of lower temperature. If two regions are at the same temperature, there is a thermal equilibrium between them and there will be no net heat transfer between them. Conduction is a form of heat transfer that requires contact. Since heat is a measure of kinetic energy, most commonly vibration, at the atomic level, it may be transferred from one location to another or one object to another by contact. The rate at which heat is transferred is proportional to the material's thermal conductivity k, cross-sectional area A, and temperature gradient dT/dx, $q = kA(dT/dx)$. If two ends of a rod are each held at a constant temperature, the heat transfer through the rod will be given as $q = kA(T_H - T_L)/d$, where d is the length of the rod. The heat will flow from the hot end to the cold end. The thermal conductivity is generally given in units of W/m-K. Metals are some of the best conductors, many having a thermal conductivity around 400 W/m-K. The thermal conductivity of wood is very small, generally less than 0.5 W/m-k. Diamond is extremely thermally conductive and may have a conductivity of over 2,000 W/m-k. Although fluids also have thermal conductivity, they will tend to transfer heat primarily through convection.

Convection

Heat always flows from a region of higher temperature to a region of lower temperature. If two regions are at the same temperature, there is a thermal equilibrium between them and there will be no net heat transfer between them. Convection is a mode of heat transfer in which a surface in contact with a fluid experiences a heat flow. The heat rate for convection is given as $q = hA\Delta T$, where h is the convection coefficient. The convection coefficient is dependent on a number of factors, including the configuration of the surface and the nature and velocity of the fluid. For complicated configurations, it often has to be determined experimentally.

Convection may be classified as either free or forced. In free convection, when a surface transfers heat to the surrounding air, the heated air becomes less dense and rises, allowing cooler air to descend and come into contact with the surface. Free convection may also be called natural convection. Forced convection in this example would involve forcibly cycling the air: for instance, with a fan. While this does generally require an additional input of work, the convection coefficient is always greater for forced convection.

Radiation

Heat always flows from a region of higher temperature to a region of lower temperature. If two regions are at the same temperature, there is a thermal equilibrium between them and there will be no net heat transfer between them. Radiation heat transfer occurs via electromagnetic radiation between two bodies. Unlike conduction and convection, radiation requires no medium in which to take place. Indeed, the heat we receive from the sun is entirely radiation since it must pass through a vacuum to reach us. Every body at a temperature above absolute zero emits heat radiation at a rate given by the equation $q = e\sigma AT^4$, where e is the surface emissivity and σ is the Stefan-Boltzmann constant. The net radiation heat-transfer rate for a body is given by $q = e\sigma A(T^4 - T_0^4)$, where T_0 is the temperature of the surroundings. Emissivity, which has a value between 0 and 1, is a measure of how well a surface absorbs and emits radiation. Dark-colored surfaces tend to have high emissivity, while shiny or reflective surfaces have low emissivity. In the radiation heat-rate equation, it is important to remember to use absolute temperature units, since the temperature value is being raised to a power.

Kinetic molecular theory and the ideal gas law

The kinetic molecular theory of gases states that the pressure exerted by a gas is due to numerous collisions of molecules with one another and with container walls. This assertion led to the development of what is now known as the ideal gas law: $PV = nRT$, where P is pressure, V is volume, T is temperature, n is the number of moles of gas present, and R is the universal gas constant. Different aspects of this law have different names, but there are many simple relations that may be derived from it. For instance, if an ideal gas is contained such that no molecules can escape, then it may be said that $P_1V_1/T_1 = P_2V_2/T_2$, where the subscripts indicate distinct sets of conditions. Generally, one of the three variables will be held constant while the other two change. If an ideal gas in a container with a constant volume is heated, the effect this has on the pressure can be determined both analytically and numerically. Additional energy imparted to the gas particles will cause them to move faster and, by the kinetic molecular theory, faster particles mean more collisions and a higher resulting pressure. Numerically, $P_1/T_1 = P_2/T_2$. This means that if T_2 is higher than T_1, then P_2 must be equivalently higher than P_1 to maintain the same ratio. Other derivations from the ideal gas law include calculating molarity or moles per unit volume ($n/V = P/RT$), gas density if the molecular weight M is known ($\rho = PM/RT$), or conversely, molecular weight if the density is known ($M = \rho RT/P$).

Heat engines and the Carnot cycle

A heat engine is a mechanical device that takes in heat energy Q_H from a high-temperature region, uses that energy to produce work W, and then expels heat Q_C to a lower-temperature region. When the machine is operating at steady state, such that it does not change temperature, the first law of thermodynamics tells us that the net heat input is equal to the work achieved, $Q_H - Q_C = W$. We can define the efficiency of a heat engine as the work received divided by the work put in, or $\eta = W/Q_H$. The rejected heat Q_C is not considered work received because it is not usable for work. The efficiency may also be calculated as $\eta = 1 - Q_C/Q_H$. From this, we can see that 100% efficiency can only be achieved if $Q_C = 0$. However, constructing a heat engine that expels no heat is impossible.

A Carnot engine is a heat engine that operates on the Carnot cycle, an ideal reversible gas cycle that consists of the following processes: high-temperature isothermal expansion, adiabatic expansion, low-temperature isothermal compression, and adiabatic compression. The efficiency of this ideal engine is given as $\eta = 1 - T_C/T_H$, where T_C and T_H are the low and high temperatures of the gas during the cycle. Carnot's theorem states that no heat engine operating between T_C and T_H can have a higher efficiency than that of the Carnot engine.

Thermodynamic processes of gases

In discussing thermodynamic processes applied to gases, it is important to understand what is meant by some of the different types of processes that can take place. Most real processes do not strictly hold to one of these types, but most can be reasonably approximated by one of them. A process in which the pressure remains constant is known as an isobaric process. In this type of process, the volume-to-absolute-temperature ratio remains constant. In an isothermal process, the temperature remains constant, as does the product of the pressure and volume. For isothermal processes, the internal energy of the gas is constant and, by the first law of thermodynamics, the heat added is equal to the work done by the gas. An adiabatic process is one in which no heat is transferred between the gas or its surroundings. This does not mean that the temperature of the gas remains the same, but only that any temperature changes are due to changes in pressure or volume or, by the first law, the change in internal energy of the gas is equal to the amount of work done on the gas by its surroundings.

Laws of thermodynamics

The law of conservation of energy states that in a closed system, energy cannot be created or destroyed but only changed from one form to another. This is also known as the first law of thermodynamics. Another way to state this is that the total energy in an isolated system is constant. Energy comes in many forms that may be transformed from one kind to another, but in a closed system, the total amount of energy is conserved or remains constant. For example, potential energy can be converted in kinetic energy, thermal energy, radiant energy, or mechanical energy. In an isolated chemical reaction, there can be no energy created or destroyed. The energy simply changes forms.

The second law of thermodynamics is a statement of the natural tendency of all things toward disorder rather than order. It deals with a quantity called entropy, which is an inverse measure of the remaining useful energy in a system. If we take a system of a pot of hot water and an ice cube, the system entropy initially has a value of s_1. After the ice cube melts in the water and the system reaches an equilibrium temperature, the system has larger entropy value s_2, which is the maximum entropy for the system. The system cannot return to its initial state without work input to refreeze the ice cube and reheat the water. If this is done and the system returns to a state with entropy s_1, then the entropy of the surroundings must at the same time increase by more than $s_2 - s_1$, since the net entropy from any process is always greater than zero. Reversible processes are those that may be accomplished in reverse without requiring additional work input. These processes do not exist in the real world, but can be useful for approximating some situations. All real processes are irreversible, meaning they require additional work input to accomplish in reverse. Another important concept is that of spontaneity, the ability of a process to occur without instigation. An ice cube located in an environment at a temperature above the freezing point will melt. Although some processes can decrease system entropy at a cost to the entropy of the surroundings, all spontaneous processes involve an increase in system entropy.

The third law of thermodynamics regards the behavior of systems as they approach absolute zero temperature. Actually reaching a state of absolute zero is impossible. According to this law, all activity disappears as molecules slow to a standstill near absoulte zero, and the system achieves a perfect crystal structure while the system entropy approaches its minimum value. For most systems, this would in fact be a value of zero entropy. Note that this does not violate the second law since causing a system to approach absolute zero would require an immense increase in the entropy of the surroundings, resulting in a positive net entropy. This law is used to determine the value of a material's standard entropy, which is its entropy value at the standard temperature of 25 °C.

The zeroth law of thermodynamics deals with thermal equilibrium between two systems. It states that if two systems are both in thermal equilibrium with a third system, then they are in thermal equilibrium with each other. This may seem intuitive, but it is an important basis for the other thermodynamic laws.

Energy conversion

There are many different types of energy that exist. These include mechanical, sound, magnetic, electrical, light, heat, and chemical. From the first law of thermodynamics, we know that no energy can be created or destroyed, but it may be converted from one form to another. This does not mean that all forms of energy are useful. Indeed, the second law states that net useful energy decreases in every process that takes place. Most often this occurs when other forms of energy are converted to heat through means such as friction. In these cases, the heat is quickly absorbed into the surroundings and becomes unusable. There are many examples of energy conversion, such as in an automobile. The chemical energy in the gasoline is converted to mechanical energy in the engine. Subsequently, this mechanical energy is converted to kinetic energy as the car moves. Additionally, the mechanical energy is converted to electrical energy to power the radio, headlights, air conditioner, and other devices. In the radio, electrical energy is converted to sound energy. In the headlights, it is converted to heat and light energy. In the air conditioner, it does work to remove heat energy from the car's interior. It is important to remember that, in all of these processes, a portion of the energy is lost from its intended purpose.

Vectors

Vectors are mathematical quantities with both magnitude and direction. A vector is most commonly described by the magnitude of its components in the relevant coordinate system. Vectors may exist in any number of dimensions, but for applications in mechanics they will most often be in either two or three. A vector is generally denoted by a letter either in boldface type or with an arrow above it.

Adding or subtracting vectors is as simple as adding or subracting their components. For instance, given the two vectors **a** = <1,5,7> and **b** = <5,-3,3>, **a** + **b** = <(1+5),(5−3),(7+3)> = <6,2,10>. If vectors are given as a length and an angle, it may be necessary to use trigonometry to convert these to orthogonal components.

Visually, adding a vector is accomplished by drawing the second vector starting from the endpoint of the first vector. To visually subtract a vector, draw both vectors starting from the origin. The difference will be the vector from the endpoint of the second to the endpoint of the first. Vector addition has many of the same relevant properties as scalar addition. It is commutative, in that **a** + **b** = **b** + **a**, and associative, in that (**a** + **b**) + **c** = **a** + (**b** + **c**).

Multiplication and division of vectors and scalars

There are a few different ways to multiply vectors, though none of them is exactly the same as algebraic multiplication. For instance, one way to multiply vectors is to multiply a vector by a scalar. If we are to multiply vector **a** by scalar s, we can only multiply the magnitude of **a** by the absolute value of s. The direction of the product will be the same as **a** so long as s is positive; if s is negative, the resulting vector will be in the opposite direction. To divide by s, we would simply multiply **a** by 1/s. One common example of this kind of operation in physics is in the equation for force. To find force, we multiply mass (scalar) by acceleration (vector). Of course, since mass will always be positive, the direction of the resulting vector (force) will always be in the direction of the acceleration.

Dot products

There are two different methods for multiplying two vectors: one way yields a vector product, and one way yields a scalar product. If we take the vectors **a** and **b** and decide to solve for a scalar product, we will set up this equation: $\mathbf{a} \cdot \mathbf{b} = ab \cos \varphi$. In this equation, a is the magnitude of the vector **a**, b is the magnitude of the vector **b**, and φ is the angle between **a** and **b**. Another way to arrive at the same scalar product is to multiply each component of one vector by the corresponding component in the other vector and sum the results: $\mathbf{a} \cdot \mathbf{b} = a_x b_x + a_y b_y + a_z b_z$. Since there are only scalars on the right side of the equation, the resulting product will be a scalar. This product is often referred to as a dot product, since the left side of the equation is often written with the expression, "**a** · **b**" (a dot b). This kind of equation is exemplified by the formula for work, in which a scalar (work) is found by multiplying two vectors (force and displacement).

Cross products

When two vectors are being multiplied for a vector product ($\mathbf{a} \times \mathbf{b} = \mathbf{c}$), the equation will be written $\mathbf{c} = ab \sin \varphi$, where φ is the smaller of the two angles between **a** and **b**. Because in this form the multiplication of **a** and **b** is indicated with the ×, this resulting vector is often known as the cross product. Of course, if **a** and **b** are parallel, then **a** x **b** = 0. The direction of **c** will be perpendicular to the plane that contains both **a** and **b** by the right-hand rule. It should be noted that the commutative law does not apply to this kind of multiplication. Instead, we may say that the cross product is an anticommutative function, meaning that **b** x **a** = -**a** x **b**. This kind of equation will be used in the formula for torque. An alternative method for calculating the cross product is to take the determinant of a 3x3 matrix composed of the two vectors along with the unit vectors **i**, **j**, and **k**. For vectors **a** = <2,3,6>, **b** = <1,1,4>:

$$a \times b = \begin{vmatrix} i & j & k \\ 2 & 3 & 6 \\ 1 & 1 & 4 \end{vmatrix} = i(12-6) + j(6-8) + k(2-3)$$

So **a** x **b** = 6**i** – 2**j** – **k**. Conversely, **b** x **a** = -6**i** + 2**j** + **k**.

Position

In order to determine anything about the motion of an object, we must first locate it. In other words, we must be able to describe its position relative to some reference point, often called an *origin*. If we consider the origin as the zero point of an axis, then the positive direction of the axis will be the direction in which measuring numbers are getting larger, and the negative direction is that in which the numbers are getting smaller. If a particle is located 5 cm from the origin in the positive direction of the x-axis, its location is said to be x = 5 cm. If another particle is 5 cm from the origin in the negative direction of the x-axis, its position is x = -5 cm. These two particles are 10 cm apart. A vector whose starting point is the origin and whose endpoint is the location of an object is that object's position vector, with units of length.

Displacement

When something changes its location from one place to another, it is said to have undergone *displacement*. If we can determine the original and final position of the object, then we can determine the total displacement with this simple equation: *Δx = final position – original position*. If the object has moved in the positive direction, then the final position will be greater than the original position, so we can say that the change was positive. If the final position is less than the original, however, displacement will be negative. Displacement along a straight line is a very simple example of a vector quantity: that is, it has both a magnitude and a direction. If an object travels from position x = -5 cm to x = 5 cm, it has undergone a displacement of 10 cm. If it traverses the same path in the opposite direction, its displacement is -10 cm. A vector that spans the object's displacement in the direction of travel is known as a displacement vector, with units of length.

Average velocity

There are two types of velocity that are commonly considered in physics: average velocity and instantaneous velocity. If we want to calculate the *average velocity* of an object, we must know two things. First, we must know its displacement, or the distance it has covered. Second, we must know the time it took to cover this distance. Once we have this information, the formula for average velocity is quite simple: $v_{av} = (x_f - x_i)/(t_f - t_i)$, where the subscripts i and f denote the intial and final values of the position and time. In other words, the average velocity is equal to the change in position divided by the change in time. This calculation will indicate the average distance that was covered per unit of time. Average velocity is a vector and will always point in the same direction as the displacement vector (since time is a scalar and always positive).

Instantaneous velocity

There are two types of velocity that are commonly considered in physics: average velocity and instantaneous velocity. In order to obtain the *instantaneous velocity* of an object, we must find its average velocity and then try to decrease Δt as close as possible to zero. As Δt decreases, it approaches what is known as a *limiting value*, bringing the average velocity very close to the instantaneous velocity. Instantaneous velocity is most easily discussed in the context of calculus-based physics.

Acceleration

Acceleration is the change in the velocity of an object. Like velocity, acceleration may be computed as an average or an instantaneous quantity. To calculate average acceleration, we may use this simple equation: $a_{av} = \frac{v_f - v_i}{t_f - t_i}$, where the subscripts *i* and *f* denote the initial and final values of the velocity and time. The so-called instantaneous acceleration of an object can be found by reducing the time component to the limiting value until instantaneous velocity is approached. Acceleration will be expressed in units of distance divided by time squared; for instance, meters per second squared. Like position and velocity, acceleration is a vector quantity and will therefore have both magnitude and direction.

Constant acceleration

The phenomenon of constant acceleration allows physicists to construct a number of helpful equations. Perhaps the most fundamental equation of an object's motion is the position equation: $x = at^2/2 + v_it + x_i$. If the object is starting from rest at the origin, this equation reduces to $x = at^2/2$. The position equation can be rearranged to give the displacement equation: $\Delta x = at^2/2 + v_it$. If the object's acceleration is unknown, the position or displacement may be found by the equation $\Delta x = (v_f + v_i)t/2$. If the position of an object is unknown, the velocity may be found by the equation $v = v_i + at$. Similarly, if the time is unknown, the velocity after a given displacement may be found by the equation $v = \text{sqrt}(v_i^2 + 2a\Delta x)$.

Uniform circular motion

We may say that a particle is in *uniform circular motion* when it is traveling in a circle, or circular arc, and at a constant speed. Crucially, we must note that such a particle is accelerating, even though the magnitude of its velocity does not change. This is because velocity is a vector, and consequently, any change in its direction is an acceleration. So, if we take two points on an arc of radius, r, separated by an angle, θ, and want to determine the time it will take a particle to move between these two points at a constant speed, $|v|$, we can use the equation: $\Delta t = r\theta/|v|$. The quantity $|v|/r$ is often written as ω, or angular velocity, having units of radians per second, so the time may also be computed as $\Delta t = \theta/\omega$. The speed, or absolute value of the velocity, of an object in uniform circular motion is also called the tangential speed, because the object is always moving in a direction tangent to the circle. Similarly, an increase in the magnitude of this velocity is called tangential acceleration. A very important component of uniform motion is the centripetal acceleration. This is the acceleration that changes the direction of the velocity vector to follow the circular arc. It is directed toward the center of the circle or arc and is described by $a_c = |v|^2/r = r\omega^2$.

Projectile motion

When we discuss *projectile motion*, we are referring to the movement of an object through two dimensions during a free fall. Two-dimensional motion may be described using the same equations as one-dimensional motion, but two equations must be considered simultaneously. While setting up some basic equations for projectile motion, we will assume that the rate of acceleration towards the ground is g = 9.8 m/s, and that the effect of air resistance can be ignored. If a projectile is launched under such ideal conditions, we may say that its initial velocity is $\mathbf{v_0} = v_0\cos(\theta)\mathbf{i} + v_0\sin(\theta)\mathbf{j}$. These two velocity components are sometimes written as v_{x0} and v_{y0}, respectively.

Example: If a cannon located at a height of 5 m above ground level fires a cannonball 250 m/s at an angle of pi/6 from the horizontal, how far will the cannonball travel before hitting the ground?

When the cannonball hits the ground, it has been displaced by -5 m in the y-direction. Solving for the components of initial velocity yields $v_{x0} = 216.5$ m/s, $v_{y0} = 125$ m/s. Setting up the y-direction displacement equation results in the following: $-5 = 125t_f - 4.9t_f^2$. Solving for t_f yields an impact time of around 25.5 seconds. To find the horizontal distance covered, simply set up the displacement equation for the x-direction: $\Delta x = v_{x0}t_f + a_xt_f^2/2$. Since we ignore the effects of air resistance, acceleration in the x-direction is zero, yielding a flight distance of 5,530 m.

Relative motion and inertial reference frames

When we describe motion as being *relative*, we mean that it can only be measured in relation to something else. If a moving object is considered as it relates to some stationary object or arbitrary location, it will have a different measured velocity than it would if it were compared to some other object that is itself in motion. In other words, the measure of an object's velocity depends entirely on the reference frame from which the measurement is taken. When performing measurements of this kind, we may use any reference point we like. However, once we have decided on a reference point, we must be consistent in using it as the basis for all of our measurements, or else we will go astray. Additionally, if we want to be able to apply Newton's laws of motion or Galilean principles of relativity, we must select an inertial reference frame: that is, a reference frame that is not accelerating or rotating. A car traveling at a constant speed in a straight line is an inertial reference frame. A car moving in uniform circular motion is not. An object's velocity with respect to a frame fixed to the earth can be computed by measuring its velocity from any inertial reference frame and combining that velocity by vector addition with the velocity of the inertial frame with respect to the earth. For instance, if a man is traveling in the x-direction at 20 m/s, and he throws a rock out the window at a relative velocity of 15 m/s in the y-direction, the rock's velocity with respect to the earth is found by adding the two vectors: $\mathbf{v}_r = 20\mathbf{i} + 15\mathbf{j}$ m/s.

Newton's laws

Before Newton formulated his laws of mechanics, it was generally assumed that some force had to act on an object continuously in order to make the object move at a constant velocity. Newton, however, determined that unless some other force acted on the object (most notably friction or air resistance), it would continue in the direction it was pushed at the same velocity forever. In this light, a body at rest and a body in motion are not all that different, and Newton's first law makes little distinction. It states that a body at rest will tend to remain at rest, while a body in motion will tend to remain in motion. This phenomenon is commonly referred to as inertia, the tendency of a body to remain in its present state of motion. In order for the body's state of motion to change, it must be acted on by a non-zero net force. Net force is the vector sum of all forces acting on a body. If this vector sum is zero, then there is no unbalanced force, and the body will remain in its present state of motion. It is important to remember that this law only holds in inertial reference frames.

Newton's second law states that an object's acceleration is directly proportional to the net force acting on the object, and inversely proportional to the object's mass. It is generally written in equation form $\mathbf{F} = m\mathbf{a}$, where $\mathbf{F}$ is the net force acting on a body, m is the mass of the body, and $\mathbf{a}$ is its acceleration. It is important to note from this equation that since the mass is always a positive quantity, the acceleration vector is always pointed in the same direction as the net force vector. Of course, in order to apply this equation correctly, one must clearly identify the body to which it is being applied. Once this is done, we may say that $\mathbf{F}$ is the vector sum of all forces acting on that body, or the net force. This measure includes only those forces that are external to the body; any internal forces, in which one part of the body exerts force on another, are discounted. Newton's second law somewhat encapsulates his first, because it includes the principle that if no net force is acting on a body, the body will not accelerate. As was the case with his first law, Newton's second law may only be applied in inertial reference frames.

Newton's third law of motion is quite simple: for every force, there is an equal and opposite force. When a hammer strikes a nail, the nail hits the hammer just as hard. If we consider two objects, *A* and *B*, then we may express any contact between these two bodies with the equation $F_{AB} = -F_{BA}$. It is important to note in this kind of equation that the order of the subscripts denotes which body is exerting the force. Although the two forces are often referred to as the *action* and *reaction* forces, in physics there is really no such thing. There is no implication of cause and effect in the equation for Newton's third law. At first glance, this law might seem to forbid any movement at all. We must remember, however, that these equal, opposite forces are exerted on different bodies with different masses, so they will not cancel each other out.

Weight

Too often, weight is confused with mass. Strictly speaking, weight is the force pulling a body towards the center of a nearby astronomical body. Of course, in the case of most day-to-day operations for human beings, that astronomical body is the earth. The reason for weight is primarily a gravitational attraction between the masses of the two bodies. The SI unit for weight is the Newton. In general, we will be concerned with situations in which bodies with mass are located where the free-fall acceleration is g. In these situations, we may say that the magnitude of the weight vector is W = mg. As a vector, weight can be expressed as either -mg**j** or -W**j**, in which **j** is the direction on the axis pointing away from the earth.

Static and kinetic frictional forces

In order to illustrate the concept of friction, let us imagine a book resting on a table. As it sits there, the force of its weight (*W*) is equal and opposite to the normal force (*N*). If, however, we were to exert a force (*F*) on the book, attempting to push it to one side, a frictional force (*f*) would arise, equal and opposite to our force. This kind of frictional force is known as *static frictional force*. As we increase our force on the book, however, we will eventually cause it to accelerate in the direction of our force. At this point, the frictional force opposing us will be known as *kinetic frictional force*. For the most part, kinetic frictional force is lower than static frictional force, and so the amount of force needed to maintain the movement of the book will be less than that needed to initiate movement. For wheels and spherical objects on a surface, static friction at the point of contact allows them to roll, but there is a frictional force that resists the rolling motion as well, due primarily to deformation effects in the rolling material. This is known as rolling friction, and tends to be much smaller than either static or kinetic friction.

Friction

The first property of friction is that, if the body does not move when horizontal force F is applied, then the static frictional force is exactly equal and opposite to F. Static frictional force has a maximum value, however, which is expressed as $f_{s,max} = \mu_s N$, in which μ_s is the coefficient of static friction, and N is the magnitude of the normal force. If the magnitude of F should exceed the maximum value of static friction, the body will begin to move. Once the body has begun to slide, the frictional force will generally decrease. The value to which the frictional force will diminish is expressed as $f_k = \mu_k N$, in which μ_k is the coefficient of kinetic friction. For objects inclined to roll, such as balls or wheels, there is a rolling frictional force that resists the continued rolling of such an object. This force is expressed by $f_r = \mu_r N$, in which μ_r is the coefficient of rolling friction. All of these frictional coefficients are dimensionless. Since the value of the frictional force depends on the interaction of the body and the surface, it is usually described as friction between the two.

Equilibrium

We may say that an object is in a state of equilibrium when it has a constant linear momentum P at its center of mass, and when angular momentum L is also constant about the center of mass. In other words, a wheel may be in equilibrium when it is spinning at a constant speed, and a hockey puck may be in equilibrium as it slides across ice. These are both examples of dynamic equilibrium. The phrase static equilibrium, however, is reserved for objects in which both linear and angular momentum are at zero. An object sitting on a table could be considered as being in static equilibrium.

If a body is in translational equilibrium, then its linear momentum will be constant, and there will be a net force of zero. Likewise, a body in rotational equilibrium will have a constant angular momentum, and again there will be a net torque of zero. Both of these equations are vector equations, and as such are both equivalent to three scalar equations for the three dimensions of motion, though in most instances, only one or two dimensions will be considered at a time. We may say that the two requirements for a body to be in equilibrium are that the vector sum of all the external forces acting on the body must be zero, and the vector sum of all the external torques acting on the body must also be zero. Conversely, if we are told that a body is in equilibrium, we may assume that both of these conditions will hold, and that we can use them to find unknown forces or torques.

For a body in equilibrium, the net force vector and the net torque vector will both be equal to zero. For the most common cases, two-dimensional systems, these conditions can be fully expressed by one or two force summation equations and one torque summation equation. Torque summations may be taken about any point on the body, though strategic placement can make calculations simpler. To determine the torque exerted by a force, simply multiply the magnitude of the force by the perpendicular distance to the point of interest. It will be necessary to decide in advance which direction of torque (clockwise or counterclockwise) will be considered positive.

For example, if we have a bar of known mass, m, that is suspended by cables at each end and whose center of mass is two thirds of the way along its length, L, we can use the equilibrium conditions to determine the tension in each cable. Gravity exerts a force of $-mg$ on the bar's center of mass. Translational equilibrium conditions tell us that $T_1 + T_2 - mg = 0$. Setting the total torque about the center of mass equal to zero, considering counterclockwise torque to be positive, yields the equation $T_2(L/3) - T_1(2L/3) = 0$. Solving these equations results in $T_1 = mg/3$ and $T_2 = 2mg/3$. This result makes sense since the center of mass is closer to the second cable.

Polar coordinates

Polar coordinates were designed to be useful in situations in which circular arcs are more common than straight lines and right angles. Instead of having x- and y-coordinates, an object's location is described by its distance from the origin, r, and the angle between its position vector and the positive x-axis, commonly denoted as θ.

The two coordinate systems are related by the following equations:

- $x = r\cos(\theta)$, $y = r\sin(\theta)$
- $r = \text{sqrt}(x^2 + y^2)$, $\theta = \tan^{-1}(y/x)$

The direction and nature of the conversion will dictate which set of equations to use. The polar coordinate system simplifies many calculations of circular motion. Instead of a velocity in the x- or y-direction, velocity may be described by motion toward or away from the origin and an increase or decrease in the angle θ. For uniform circular motion, the change in r is zero, and the rate of change of angle θ is constant. The only acceleration on the body is the centripetal acceleration, given by $a_c = |v|^2/r = r\omega^2$, where ω is the rate of change in angle θ, known as the rotational velocity, keeping the body in its circular arc. This acceleration is caused by a centripetal force that pulls the object toward the center of the circle. By Newton's second law, this force has a magnitude given by $F = ma_c = m|v|^2/r = mr\omega^2$.

Kinetic energy

The kinetic energy of an object is that quality of its motion that can be related in a qualitative way to the amount of work performed on the object. Kinetic energy can be defined as $KE = mv^2/2$, in which m is the mass of an object and v is the magnitude of its velocity. Kinetic energy cannot be negative, since it depends on the square of velocity. Units for kinetic energy are the same as those for work: joules. Kinetic energy is a scalar quantity.

Changes in kinetic energy occur when a force does work on an object, such that the speed of the object is altered. This change in kinetic energy is equal to the amount of work that is done, and can be expressed as $W = KE_f - KE_i = \Delta KE$. This equation is commonly referred to as the work-kinetic energy theorem. If there are several different forces acting on the object, then W in this equation is simply the total work done by all the forces, or by the net force. This equation can be very helpful in solving some problems that would otherwise rely solely on Newton's laws of motion.

Power

Put simply, power is the rate at which work is done. Power, like work, is a scalar quantity. If we know the amount of work, W, that has been performed in a given amount of time, Δt, then we may find average power, $P_{av} = W/\Delta t$. If we are instead looking for the instantaneous power, there are two possibilities. If the force on an object is constant, and the object is moving at a constant velocity, then the instantaneous power is the same as the average power. If either the force or the velocity is varying, the instantaneous power should be computed by the equation $P = Fv$, where F and v are the instantaneous force and velocity. This equation may also be used to compute average power if the force and velocity are constant. Power is typically expressed in joules per second, or watts.

Work

The equation for work (W) is fairly simple: $W = F \cdot d$, where F is the force exerted and d is the displacement of the object on which the force is exerted. For the simplest case, when the vectors of force and displacement have the same direction, the work done is equal to the product of the magnitudes of the force and displacement. If force and displacement have the same direction, then work is positive; if they are in opposite directions, however, work is negative; and if they are perpendicular, the work done by the force is zero.

For example, if a man pushes a block horizontally across a surface with a constant force of 10 N for a distance of 20 m, the work done by the man is 200 N-m or 200 J. If instead the block is sliding and the man tries to slow its progress by pushing against it, his work done is -200 J, since he is pushing in the direction opposite the motion. Also, if the man pushes vertically downward on the block while it slides, his work done is zero, since his force vector is perpendicular to the displacement vector of the block. It is important to note in each of these cases that neither the mass of the block nor the elapsed time is considered when calculating the amount of work done by the man.

If the force on an object varies across the distance the object is moved, then a simple product will not yield the work. If we consider the work performed by a variable force in one dimension, then we are assuming that the directions of the force and the displacement are the same. The magnitude of the force will depend on the position of the particle. In order to calculate the amount of work performed by a variable force over a given distance, we should first divide the total displacement into a number of intervals, each with a width of Δx. We may then say that the amount of work performed during any one interval is $\Delta W = F_{av}\Delta x$, where F_{zv} is the average force over the interval Δx. We can then say that the total amount of work performed is the sum of all work performed during the various intervals. By reducing the interval to an infinitesimal length, we obtain the integral:

$$W = \int_{x_1}^{x_2} F_x dx$$

This integral requires that the force be a known function of x.

The work performed by a spring is one of the classic examples of work performed by variable force. When a spring is neither compressed nor extended, we may say that it is in a relaxed state. Any time the spring is taken out of this state, whether by being stretched or compressed, it will exert what is called a restoring force, as it attempts to return to its relaxed state. In most cases, we can say that the force, F, exerted by the spring is proportional to the displacement of the free end from its position during the relaxed state. This is known as Hooke's law, and is expressed F = -kx, where k is the spring constant or stiffness. The x-coordinate in this equation corresponds to an axis where x = 0 is the coordinate of the relaxed position. The negative sign in this equation indicates that the force is always opposite to the displacement.

If we are to move a block attached to a spring from point x_i to point x_f, we can be said to be doing work on the block, as the spring is also doing work on the block. To determine the work done by the spring on the block, we can substitute F from Hooke's law into our equation for work performed by a variable force, and arrive at this measure: $W = k(x_i^2 - x_f^2)/2$. This work will be positive if $x_i^2 > x_f^2$, and negative if the opposite is true. If $x_i = 0$ and we decide to call the final position x, then we may change our equation: $W = -kx^2/2$. It is important to keep in mind that this is the work done by the spring. The work done by the force that moves the block to its final position will be a positive quantity.

Like all simple harmonic oscillators, springs operate by storing and releasing potential energy. The amount of energy being stored or released by a spring is equal to the magnitude of the work done by the spring during that same operation. The total potential energy stored in a spring can be calculated as $PE = kx^2/2$. Neglecting the effects of friction and drag, an object oscillating on a spring will continue to do so indefinitely, since total mechanical energy (kinetic and potential) is conserved. In such a situation, the period of oscillation can be calculated as T = 2pi*sqrt(m/k).

Conservative and non-conservative forces

Forces that change the state of a system by changing kinetic energy into potential energy, or vice versa, are called conservative forces. This name arises because these forces conserve the total amount of kinetic and potential energy. Every other kind of force is considered non-conservative. One example of a conservative force is gravity. Consider the path of a ball thrown straight up into the air. Since the ball has the same amount of kinetic energy when it is thrown as it does when it returns to its original location (known as completing a closed path), gravity can be said to be a conservative force. More generally, a force can be said to be conservative if the work it does on an object through a closed path is zero. Frictional force would not meet this standard, of course, because it is only capable of performing negative work.

Simple harmonic motion

Simple harmonic motion in a single dimension, x, can be described by the equation $x = A\cos(\omega t + \varphi)$, where A is the amplitude of oscillation, ω is the angular frequency of oscillation, and φ is the phase. The particular trigonometric operator used in the equation is not of great importance as sine may be substituted for cosine given a proper modification of the phase. Graphically, the motion of a harmonic oscillator starting from rest at maximum displacement is shown by the graph below. This graph assumes no energy lost to friction or drag.

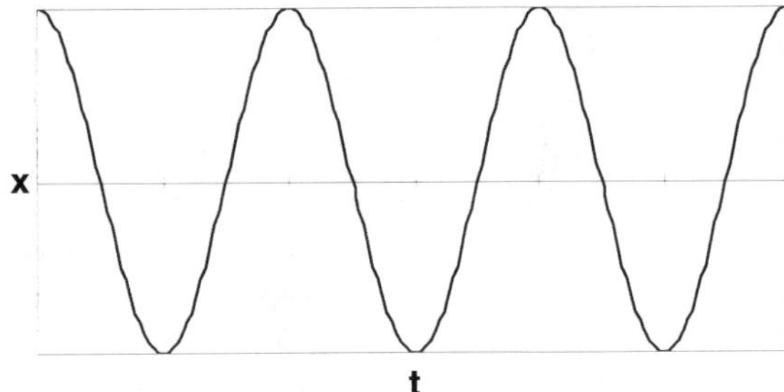

Pendulum

A pendulum is a harmonic oscillator that depends on the force of gravity for its motion. If we consider a simple pendulum composed of a mass hanging from an inelastic, massless string, then we may describe its restoring force as $F = -mg\sin(\theta)$, in which θ is the angle by which the mass is removed from its resting position. If the angle is very small, less than 15° or pi/12, then $\theta \approx \sin(\theta)$, and the motion of the pendulum is like that of a simple harmonic oscillator. If this is the case, then the period of our simple pendulum can be found as T = 2pi*sqrt(L/g), where L is the length of the string. Again, this only holds if the angular amplitude θ_{max} is very small.

Like springs, pendulums operate by converting energy between kinetic and potential. Unlike springs, the potential energy stored in pendulums is gravitational potential energy. As the mass is displaced from its resting state, its height above ground increases. The potential energy stored in a simple pendulum can be calculated as $PE = mgL(1 - \cos(\theta))$.

Linear momentum and impulse

In physics, linear momentum can be found by multiplying the mass and velocity of a particle: P = mv. Momentum has units of kg-m/s. Like velocity, momentum is a vector quantity and will always have the same direction as the velocity. Newton's second law describes momentum, stating that the rate of change of momentum is proportional to the force exerted, and is in the direction of the force. Impulse is the application of force over a period of time. If a constant net force of 10 N is exerted on an object for 5 seconds, it gives the object an impulse of 50 N-s. An impulse of 50 N-s corresponds to a change in momentum of 50 kg-m/s in the direction of the force. In equation form, $Ft = \Delta mv$, where F is a constant net force. If the force is varying, it will be necessary to integrate the force over time.

For example, suppose a 2-kg block is initially at rest on a frictionless surface and a constant net force of 8 N is exerted on the block for 5 seconds. In order to determine how fast the block is moving, we need to calculate the impulse that was given to it, Ft = 40 N-s. This means that the change in momentum of the block was 40 kg-m/s. Since the block has a mass of 2 kg, this translates to an increase in velocity of 20 m/s. Thus, the block will be traveling at 20 m/s after 5 seconds.

Linear momentum and collisions

If we assume a closed and isolated system (that is, one in which no particles leave or enter, and on which the sum of external forces is zero), then we can assume that the momentum of the system will neither increase nor decrease. That is, if we write the equation for the linear momentum of the system such that the net external force $F_{ext} = 0$, then we will find that linear momentum, P, is a constant. The equation for linear momentum is a vector equation, and as such it can be divided into component equations for each dimension.

Some of the most popular examples to demonstrate conservation of linear momentum involve two objects colliding on a frictionless surface. A perfectly elastic collision is one in which both total momentum and kinetic energy are conserved. A perfectly inelastic collision is one in which only momentum is conserved, as the two bodies combine to form a single body. Most actual collisions fall somewhere between these two extremes. Unless a collision is specified as being elastic, it should be assumed that only momentum is conserved.

One-dimensional collisions

All examples assume a frictionless surface.

If a 0.01-kg bullet traveling at 400 m/s strikes a stationary 10-kg block of wood, and buries itself in the wood, find the final velocity of the block and the bullet.

The bullet initially has 4 kg-m/s of momentum. The block of wood, beginning at rest, has no momentum. Thus, the final momentum is 4 kg-m/s. Given the new combined mass of 10.01 kg, the final velocity is approximately 0.4 m/s.

Two blocks, having masses of 10 kg and 40 kg, are traveling toward one another with velocities of -20 m/s and 10 m/s, respectively. If the collision was perfectly elastic, find the final velocities of each body. If it was perfectly inelastic, find the final velocity of the resulting single body.

For elastic collisions, two conditions hold: $KE_i = KE_f$ and $P_i = P_f$. Calculating initial conditions yields $KE_i = 4000$ J and $P_i = 200$ kg-m/s total for both blocks. Equating these to the final values of each yields $5v_{1f}^2 + 20v_{2f}^2 = 4000$ and $10v_{1f} + 40v_{2f} = 200$. Solving both equations simultaneously gives $v_{1f} = 28$ m/s and $v_{2f} = -2$ m/s.

The inelastic case is much simpler. Since the two blocks merge to form one, the final momentum, 200 kg-m/s, is divided by the combined mass to give the final velocity of 4 m/s.

Two-dimensional collisions

All examples assume a frictionless surface.

Two blocks of mass, 5 kg and 10 kg, having velocities $\mathbf{v_1} = 9\mathbf{i}$ m/s and $\mathbf{v_2} = 3\mathbf{j}$ m/s, respectively, are on a collision course. If the collision is perfectly inelastic, find the velocity of the combined block after collision.

Since each block initially has velocity in only one dimension, it is a simple calculation to find intial momentum values: P_x = 45 kg-m/s and P_y = 30 kg-m/s. With the new combined mass of 15 kg, the final velocity vector will be $\mathbf{v_f}$ = 3**i** + 2**j** m/s.

Two hockey pucks, each with a mass of 0.15 kg, having velocity vectors $\mathbf{v_1}$ = 20**i** + 30**j** m/s and $\mathbf{v_2}$ = -50**i** – 10**j** m/s, are headed toward a collision. If the final velocity of one puck is $\mathbf{v_{2f}}$ = -10**i** + 15**j** m/s, find the final velocity vector of the other puck.

We must ensure that momentum is conserved in both dimensions. The initial momentum in the x- and y-directions is calculated to be P_{xi} = -4.5 kg-m/s and P_{yi} = 3 kg-m/s. Since we know the final velocity of one of the pucks, we can find the other's final velocity to be $\mathbf{v_{1f}}$ = -20**i** + 5**j** m/s.

Angular motion and the axis of rotation

When a body is moving in a straight line, it is said to be moving in translation. When, on the other hand, it is moving around some fixed axis, it is said to be in rotation. For a rotating object, the fixed axis is called the axis of rotation. Every point on the body will move in a circle that has this axis as its center, and every point will move through the same angle over the same interval of time. Angles may be measured in one of three units: degrees, radians, or revolutions. A full rotation is equal to 360 degrees, 2pi radians, or 1 revolution. On a circle, one radian is the angle that measures an arc length equal to the radius of the circle. Since a circle's circumference is 2pi times the radius, one full rotation is equal to 2pi radians.

Angular motion has many correlations to linear motion. For an angle of rotation, θ, the linear distance traveled is $x = r\theta$. For angular velocity, ω, the linear velocity is $v = r\omega$. For angular acceleration, α, the linear acceleration is $a = r\alpha$. When discussing angular motion in this way, the angular unit is always radians.

Applying Newton's second law and other linear motion concepts to rotational motion

Newton's second law, commonly stated as F = ma, is applied to rotational motion by the equation $\tau = I\alpha$. That is, the torque is equal to the moment of inertia times the angular acceleration. Torque is calculated as the magnitude of an applied force times its perpendicular distance from the body's center of mass. A body's moment of inertia depends on both its mass and its configuration. Each particle in a body contributes a moment of $I = mr^2$, where m is the particle's mass and r is its distance from the center of mass. Thus, for a thin ring or a thin hollow sphere, the moment for the body is $I = mr^2$. Some other commonly encountered shapes are spheres ($I = (2/5)mr^2$) and disks ($I = (1/2)mr^2$). A closely related property of these shapes is the radius of gyration, k. This quantity is the average distance of mass from the center. It can be found by the equation k = sqrt(I/m). Similarly, the moment of inertia may be found as $I = mk^2$.

Another important corollary with linear motion is momentum. An object's angular momentum may be calculated as $L = I\omega$. All the same conservation rules for linear momentum apply to angular momentum as well. Additionally, there is a kinetic energy associated with rotational motion. It is calculated as $KE_r = I\omega^2/2$. When calculating kinetic energy for an object that is in both linear and angular motion, the total kinetic energy is the sum of the translational and rotational kinetic energy, $KE = mv^2/2 + I\omega^2/2$.

Applying conservation of energy and momentum to angular motion problems

A metal hoop of mass m and radius r is released from rest at the top of a hill of height h. Assuming that it rolls without sliding and does not lose energy to friction or drag, what will be the hoop's angular and linear velocities upon reaching the bottom of the hill? The hoop's initial energy is all potential energy, PE = mgh. As the hoop rolls down, all of its energy is converted to translational and rotational kinetic energy. Thus, $mgh = mv^2/2 + I\omega^2/2$. Since the moment for a hoop is $I = mr^2$, and $\omega = v/r$, the equation may be rewritten as $mgh = mv^2/2 + mr^2(v^2/r^2)/2$, which further simplifies to $mgh = mv^2$. Thus, the resulting velocity of the hoop is v_f = sqrt(gh), with an angular velocity of $\omega_f = v_f/r$. Note that if you were to forget about the energy converted to rotational motion, you would calculate a final velocity of v_f = sqrt(2gh), which is the impact velocity of an object dropped from height h. Consider a planet orbiting the sun through an elliptical orbit with small radius r_S and large radius r_L. Find the angular velocity of the planet when it is at distance r_S from the sun if its velocity at r_L is ω_L. Since the size of a planet is almost insignificant compared to the interplanetary distances, the planet may be treated as a single particle of mass m, giving it a moment about the sun of $I = mr^2$. Since the gravitational force is incapable of exerting a net torque on an object, we can assume that the planet's angular momentum about the sun is a constant. Thus, $mr_L^2\omega_L = mr_S^2\omega_S$. Solving this equation for ω_S yields $\omega_S = \omega_L(r_L^2/r_S^2)$.

Mass-energy relationship

Because mass consists of atoms, which are themselves formed of subatomic particles, there is an energy inherent in the composition of all mass. If all the atoms in a given mass were formed from their most basic particles, it would require a significant input of energy. This rest energy is the energy that Einstein refers to in his famous mass-energy relation $E = mc^2$, where c is the speed of light in a vacuum. In theory, if all the subatomic particles in a given mass were to spontaneously split apart, it would give off energy $E = mc^2$. For example, if this were to happen to a single gram of mass, the resulting outburst of energy would be $E = 9 \times 10^{13}$ J, enough energy to heat more than 200,000 cubic meters of water from the freezing point to the boiling point.

In some nuclear reactions, small amounts of mass are converted to energy. The amount of energy released can be calculated through the same relation, $E = mc^2$. Most such reactions involve mass losses on the order of 10^{-30} kg.

Newton's law of gravitation

One of Newton's major insights into the behavior of physical objects was that every object in the universe exerts an attractive force on every other body. In quantitative terms, we may say that the gravitational force with which particles attract one another is given by $F = Gm_1m_2/r^2$, in which r is the distance between the particles and G is the gravitational constant, $G = 6.672 \times 10^{-11}$ N-m^2/kg^2. Although this equation is usually applied to particles, it may also be applied to objects, assuming that they are small relative to the distance between them. Newton expressed this relation by saying that a uniform spherical shell of matter attracts a particle outside the shell as if all the shell's matter were concentrated at its center. In the case of gravitation on earth, for instance, objects behave as if the earth were a single particle located at its center, and with the mass of the entire earth. Thus, regardless of an object's distance from the surface of the earth, it can be approximated as a particle due to the effective distance from the earth's center of mass. The difference in the gravitational pull on an object at sea level and that same object at the highest point on the earth's surface is about a quarter of a percent. Thus, the gravitational acceleration anywhere on the earth's surface is considered to be a constant, $g = 9.81$ m/s^2. For an object orbiting the earth, its period of orbit can be found by equating the gravitational force to the centripetal force, giving the equation $Gm_em/r^2 = mr\omega^2 = mr(2pi/T)^2$. Solving for the period yields $T = sqrt(4pi^2r^3/Gm_e)$.

Kepler's law of orbits for planets and satellites

Kepler's first law describing the movement of planets states that all planets move in elliptical orbits, with the sun at one focus. If we are to consider the motion of one planet around the sun, we will assume that its mass is much smaller than that of the sun, such that the center of mass of the system is almost in the middle of the sun. The orbit of the planet will then be defined by the semimajor axis, a (that is, half the length of the ellipse), the semiminor axis, b (half the width of the ellipse), and the eccentricity, e (the degree to which the orbit is not circular, $e = sqrt(1-b^2/a^2)$). The orbits of the planets are only slightly elliptical, though they are often exaggerated on diagrams. In a planetary orbit, the distance from the center of the ellipse to either focus is d = ae. The maximum and minimum distances of a planet from the sun are given by $r_{max} = b^2/(a - d)$ and $r_{min} = b^2/(a + d)$.

Kepler's law of areas and law of periods for planets and satellites

Kepler's second law for planets and satellites states that any line connecting a planet to the sun will sweep out equal areas in equal times, regardless of where the planet is in its orbit. In other words, the planet will move most slowly when it is far away from the sun, and fastest when it is closest. This law says basically the same thing as the law of conservation of angular momentum.

Kepler's third law for planets states that the square of the period of any planet is proportional to the cube of the semimajor axis of its orbit. This relation can be expressed $T^2 = (4pi^2/Gm)r^3$. The quantity in parentheses in this equation is a constant, its only variable being the mass of the central body. This equation holds up for elliptical orbits as well.

Fluids

It sounds obvious, perhaps, but fluids can best be defined as substances that flow. A fluid will conform, slowly or quickly, to any container in which it is placed. This is because a fluid is unable to maintain a force tangential to its surface. In other words, fluids cannot withstand shearing stress. They can, on the other hand, exert a force perpendicular to their surface. Both liquids and gases are considered to be fluids. Fluids, essentially, are those substances in which the atoms are not arranged in any permanent, rigid way. In ice, for instance, molecules are all lined up in a crystalline lattice, while in water and steam the only intermolecular arrangements are haphazard connections between neighboring molecules.

The density of a fluid is generally expressed with the symbol ρ. The density may be found with the simple equation $\rho = m/V$, mass per unit volume. Density is a scalar property, meaning that it has no direction component. It is typically measured in SI units of kilograms per cubic meter. While the density of a gas will tend to fluctuate considerably depending on the level of pressure, the density of a liquid is comparatively stable. The density of water is most often taken to be 1000 kg/m^3.

The pressure of a fluid is calculated as P = F/A, force per unit area. To find the pressure at a given depth in a fluid, or the hydrostatic pressure, the pressure can be calculated as $P = \rho gh$, where h is the fluid depth. Pressure, like fluid density, is a scalar, and does not have a direction. The equation for pressure is concerned only with the magnitude of that force, not with the direction in which it is pointing. The SI unit of pressure is the Newton per square meter, or pascal.

Pascal's principle

Pascal's principle states that a change in the pressure applied to an enclosed fluid is transmitted undiminished to every portion of the fluid, as well as to the walls of the containing vessel. Imagine, for instance, a container filled with liquid, on top of which rests a piston loaded down with a lead weight. The atmosphere, lead weight, and piston will combine to exert pressure P_{ext} on the liquid, so the total pressure will be $P = P_{ext} + \rho gh$, for every point at height h within the fluid. Imagine again, an enclosed fluid in a container with two pistons on top, one with area $A_1 = 2\ m^2$ and the other with area $A_2 = 4\ m^2$. Since the pressure will be the same at both pistons, the upward force on the larger piston will be twice that of the smaller, since it has a larger area and the force is equal to the pressure times the area over which it is applied.

Archimedes' principle

If an object is submerged in water, it will have a buoyant force exerted on it in the upward direction. This force is caused by the water pressure acting on the bottom surface of the object. The deeper the object is submerged, the greater the pressure at the bottom surface. Often, of course, this buoyant force is much too small to keep an object from sinking to the bottom. This idea of buoyancy is summarized in Archimedes' principle: a body wholly or partially submerged in a fluid will be buoyed up by a force equal to the weight of the fluid displaced by the body. Thus, an object's ability to remain afloat in a fluid depends on its density relative to that of the fluid. If the fluid has a higher density than the object, it will float. Otherwise, it will sink. This principle can also be used to find the weight of a floating object by calculating the volume of fluid that it has displaced. For instance if a cube with a volume of $1\ m^3$ is floating in water to a depth of 0.25 m, the cube is displacing $0.25\ m^3$ of water. This is the equivalent of 250 kg of water, creating a buoyancy force of 2450 N. Thus, the block weighs 2450 N, has a mass of 250 kg, and has a density of $250\ kg/m^3$.

Ideal fluids in motion

Since the motion of actual fluids is extremely complex, physicists usually refer to ideal fluids when they make their calculations. Using ideal fluids in equations is a bit like discounting friction in other calculations; it tends to make the process more mathematically manageable. So, when we deal with ideal fluids, we are making four assumptions. First, we are assuming that the flow is steady; in other words, the velocity of every part of the fluid is the same. Second, we assume that fluids are incompressible, and therefore have a consistent density. Third, we assume that fluids are nonviscous, meaning that they flow easily and without resistance. Finally, we assume that the flow of ideal fluids is irrotational: that is, particles in the fluid will not rotate around a center of mass.

Bernoulli's equation

Let us imagine an ideal fluid in a tube of flow. By applying the law of conservation of energy with ideal fluid assumptions, we can arrive at what is known as Bernoulli's equation: $P + \rho gh + \rho v^2/2 = C$, where C is a constant for a given tube of flow. Basically, this equation states that in the absence of an external input of energy or a significant elevation change, any increase in velocity will require a decrease in fluid pressure. And under similar circumstances, an increase in pressure will necessarily cause a decrease in velocity. It is essentially just a reformulation of the law of conservation of mechanical energy for fluid mechanics. Bernoulli's principle is used to explain a number of physical phenomena, including the lift force on the wings of an aircraft.

Streamlines, tube of flow, volume flow rate, and the equation of continuity

A streamline is the path traced out by a very small unit of fluid, which we will refer to as a particle. Although the velocity of a particle may change in both magnitude and direction, streamlines will never cross one another. In many instances of flow, several streamlines will group together to form what is called a tube of flow. If we were to make two cross-sections of a tube of flow, with areas A_1 and A_2, we would find that since fluid is incompressible, the same amount of fluid passes through the two cross-sections over the same interval of time. This is expressed by the equation $Q = Av$, in which Q is known as the volumetric flow rate and is constant for a given tube of flow. This equation is known as the equation of continuity; it suggests that flow will be faster in areas of the tube that are narrower. One very important equation derived from this principle is $A_1v_1 = A_2v_2$. Given that a pipe narrows its cross-section from A_1 to A_2, and the fluid velocity in A_1 is v_1, the velocity in A_2 must be $v_2 = A_1v_1/A_2$. Also important to note is that the mass flow rate is directly related to the volumetric flow rate by the equation $m_{flow} = \rho vA = \rho Q$.

Individuals of historical significance who made contributions to physics

Archimedes (ancient Greece)
Archimedes designed the compound pulley, articulated the principles of the lever, and made important contributions to engineering and geometry, calculating the area of a sphere and an ellipse and approximating the value of pi. Archimedes' Law of the Lever states that when objects are set at distances reciprocally proportional to their respective weights, they are in equilibrium.

Robert Boyle (Irish, 17th century)
Though regarded as the first modern chemist, Boyle also distinguished himself in physics and contributed to experimental design. Boyle's Law is a mathematical expression of the relationship between volume and pressure within an ideal gas.

Galileo Galilei (Italian, 17th century)
Galileo determined that all bodies, regardless of mass, fall at the same rate. He argued that motion is continuous, changed only when an external force is applied to it (later incorporated in Newton's laws of motion). His work in astronomy was important in confirming Copernicus' heliocentric model of the solar system. His principle of relativity states that the laws of physics are constant within a constantly moving system, a theory that became central to Einstein's work on relativity.

Sir Isaac Newton (English, 17th/18th century)
Newton, one of the most important scientists of all time, made critical breakthroughs in the understanding of scientific methods, motion, and optics. Newton described universal gravitation, observed that white light contains the entire spectrum of colors, and discovered the calculus independently of Leibniz (who is credited with it). The three Newtonian laws of motion are:

- An object in motion (or at rest) remains in motion (or at rest) unless acted upon by an external force.
- Force equals mass times acceleration.
- For every action, there is an equal and opposite reaction.

Amedeo Avogadro (Italian, 18th century)
Avogadro established the principles of molarity, clarified the relationship between atoms and molecules, and formalized what became known as Avogadro's principle: that equal volumes of gases held at the same pressure and temperature will contain an equal number of molecules, and

that their masses will be proportionate to their respective molecular weights. Avogadro's constant is the number of particles present in 1 mole of any substance.

Michael Faraday (English, 18th/19th century)
Faraday's most important work was in the fields of electromagnetism and electrochemistry. His work led directly to some of the most important breakthroughs in electrical technology of the twentieth century. Faraday introduced the concept of fields to the study of magnetism and electricity. He discovered what would become known as the Faraday Effect, the effect of a strong magnetic field on the behavior of light rays. The Farad (the SI unit of capacitance) and the Faraday constant (the amount of charge on one mole of electrons) are both named for him.

Marie Curie (Polish/French, 19th century)
Curie was the foremost pioneer of radioactivity. She isolated the radioactive elements polonium and radium, and established that radioactivity was a property of an atom itself rather than of the relationship between multiple molecules.

Wilhelm Ostwald (Latvian, 19th/20th century)
One of the founders of classical physical chemistry, Ostwald did important work on the properties of atomic particles, and defined a mole as the molecular weight, in grams, of a given substance.

J. Robert Oppenheimer (American, 20th century)
Oppenheimer's scientific contributions are in astrophysics, nuclear physics, and quantum field theory. He served as scientific director of the Manhattan Project, which constructed the first atomic bomb.

Linus Pauling (American, 20th century)
Pauling applied new discoveries in quantum mechanics to the field of chemistry, pioneering the study of molecular medicine. He researched the biochemical origins of genetic diseases like sickle-cell anemia.

Enrico Fermi (Italian/American, 20th century)
Fermi discovered the process of making elements artificially radioactive by bombarding them with neutrons. He divided elements into the two groups of fermions and bosons. His work on nuclear reactions led him to participate in the Manhattan Project.

Niels Bohr (Danish, 20th century)
Bohr established that the number of electrons determined the atom's chemical properties. He articulated the organization of electrons, in discrete orbits around an atom's nucleus, and that electrons could move orbits, thereby emitting radiation—the basis for quantum theory. Bohr worked on the Manhattan Project along with Oppenheimer and Fermi.

Albert Einstein (German, 20th century)
Einstein, the most famous twentieth-century scientist, was a theoretical physicist whose special theory of relativity describes the relationship of time and space, and mass and gravity. In it, he declared that gravity is a consequence of the properties of space-time and that the speed of light is constant. He hypothesized that electromagnetic energy can be absorbed or expelled by matter in quanta, and discovered the photoelectric effect.

Stephen Hawking (English, 20th/21st century)
Hawking's principal fields of research are theoretical cosmology and quantum gravity. Expanding on Einstein's work, he has hypothesized about the physical properties of black holes, described conditions necessary for a singularity, and made important contributions in string theory, in an attempt to generalize Einstein's special theory of relativity.

Waves, Electricity, and Magnetism

Coulomb's law

If two particles have charge magnitudes q_1 and q_2, and are separated by distance r, then the electrostatic force of attraction or repulsion between them can be calculated as $F = kq_1q_2/r^2$, in which k is a constant, approximately 9×10^9 N-m^2/C^2. This is known as Coulomb's law. We should note the similarity to Newton's equation for the gravitational force between two particles, $F = Gm_1m_2/r^2$. The main difference between these two equations is that while electrical force may be attractive or repulsive, gravitational force is always attractive. No experiment has ever contradicted Coulomb's law, even those conducted at the subatomic level. The constant k in the equation is called Coulomb's constant or the electrostatic constant. An important principle when calculating electrostatic force, if more than two particles are involved, is the law of superposition. If we are looking for the force exerted on a particle by two or more other particles, we must determine the individual force from each of the other particles, and take the vector sum of those forces to determine the total effect.

Electric field equation

In order to define a particular electric field, we may place an object with positive charge, q_0, called a test charge, somewhere near the charged particle, and then measure the force exerted on the object. We may then say that electric field E at that point is $E = F/q_0$. Electric field is a vector, and the direction of E will be the direction of the force acting on the test charge. If we want to fully define some region of an electric field, we must find measures for electric field at every point within that region. The SI units for electric field are Newtons per coulomb. When performing this operation, we will assume that the presence of the test charge does not affect in any way the charge distribution of the electric field.

Electrical potential energy and electric potential

Electric potential energy is the energy stored in a charge by virtue of its proximity to other charged regions. It can be calculated in the same way as calculating the amount of work required to move it to that location from an infinite distance away. The work required to move a charge of magnitude q from infinity to a distance r from another charge of magnitude Q is calculated to be $PE_e = W = kQq/r$, where k is the electrostatic constant.

Electric potential, V, is closely related to electric potential energy. The potential due to a charge Q can be found by dividing the electric potential energy of another charge q by its magnitude, $V = PE_e/q$, or by the equation $V = kQ/r$.

The difference between the electric potential of two points is known as voltage. It is measured in volts, or joules per coulomb. Since it is impractical to find a point of zero absolute electric potential, for each system a reference point or ground is defined, to which all other points in the system may be related.

Electric flux and Gauss's Law

Flux is a concept that is applicable in many areas of science. It is a measure of flow through a given area. Electric flux, Φ, is a measure of the electric field flowing perpendicularly through a particular area. It can be calculated by the equation $\Phi = E \cdot A = EA\cos(\theta)$, where θ is the angle between the direction of E and the normal vector of A.

Gauss's law states that the electric flux through an enclosing surface is directly related to charge enclosed by the surface. This relation is given by the equation $\Phi = Q/\varepsilon_0$, where ε_0 is a constant known as the permittivity of free space. The shape of the enclosing surface should be chosen to accommodate the finding of E·A. Most often, this will be a sphere or cylinder, since these surfaces are perpendicular to field lines emanating from a point or line charge, respectively. Combining the two equations yields the relation, $Q/\varepsilon_0 = E \cdot A$. Units for electric flux are $N\text{-}m^2/C$.

Conductors, insulators, and semiconductors

In many materials, electrons are able to move freely; these are known as conductors. Due to their atomic structure and delocalized electrons, metals tend to be the best conductors, particularly copper and silver. Highly conductive wires are instrumental in creating low-resistance pathways for electrons to travel along within a circuit.

Other materials naturally inhibit the movement of charge and are known as insulators. Their electrons are tightly held by the individual constituent atoms. Glass, pure water, wood, and plastic are all insulators. Insulators are necessary in circuits to prevent charge from excaping to undesirable places, such as an operator's hand. For this reason, most highly conductive materials are covered by insulators.

Semiconductors, as the name suggests, are materials that only partially conduct electrical charge. The elements silicon and germanium are both common semiconductors, and are frequently used in microelectronic devices because they allow for tight control of the rate ofconduction. In many cases, the conduction ability of semiconductors can be controlled by adjusting the temperature of the material.

Transferring electrical charge

Charge is transferred in three common ways: conduction, induction, and friction. Conduction, as the name implies, takes place between conductive materials. There must be a point of contact between the two materials and a potential difference, such as when a battery is connected to a circuit. Induction also requires conductive materials. It occurs due to one material encountering a varying magnetic field. This can be the result of a changing magnetic field or the material moving within a constant magnetic field. Charge transfer due to friction does not require conductive materials. When two materials are rubbed together, electrons may be transferred from one to the other, leaving the two materials with equal and opposite charges. This is observed when shoes are dragged across a carpeted floor.

Electromotive force and common EMF devices

A force that maintains a potential difference between two locations in a circuit is known as an electromotive force. A device that creates this force is referred to as an EMF device. The most common EMF device is the battery. Batteries operate by converting chemical energy stored in the electrolyte, the internal chemical material, into electrical energy. The reaction causes an abundance of electrons on the cathode, and when the circuit is connected, they flow to the anode, creating a flow of current. The electrolyte's composition also determines whether the battery is classified as acidic or alkaline, and wet or dry. Another EMF device is the photocell, also commonly called the solar cell, since most photocells are powered by the sun. These operate by absorbing photons, which cause the electrons to be excited and flow in a current, a process of converting light energy into electrical energy. A third type of EMF device is the generator. This device converts mechanical energy to electrical energy. A generator may be powered by such diverse sources as gasoline engines, flowing water, or even manually powered cranks. These devices utilize a rotating shaft to spin a coil within a magnetic field, creating a potential difference by induction.

Electric current

An electric current is simply an electric charge in motion. Electric current cannot exist unless there is a difference in electric potential. If, for instance, we have an isolated conducting loop, it will be at the same potential throughout. If, however, we insert a battery into this loop, then the conducting loop will no longer be at a single electric potential. A flow of electrons will result and will very quickly reach a steady state. At that point, it will be completely analogous to steady-state fluid flow. A current is quantified by the amount of charge that is transferred in a given amount of time. The SI unit for current is the ampere (A), equal to a coulomb of charge per second.

Resistors and Ohm's Law

If we were to apply the exact same potential difference between the ends of two geometrically similar rods, one made of copper and one made of glass, we would create vastly different currents. This is because these two substances have different resistances. Ohm's Law describes the relation between applied voltage and induced current, $V = IR$. This is one of the most important tools of circuit analysis. Resistance, then, can be calculated as $R = V/I$. The SI unit for resistance is the ohm (Ω), equal to a volt per ampere. When a conductor is placed into a circuit to provide a specific resistance, it is known as a resistor. For a given potential difference, the greater the resistance is to the current, the smaller the current will be. If we wish to look instead at the quality of the material of which the resistor is made, then we must consider resistivity. Resistivity, ρ, is a physical property of every material, which, if known, can be used to size a resistor for a specific resistance. Resistance is dictated by both the material and the dimensions of the resistor, given by the relation $R = \rho L/A$, where L is the effective length of the resistor and A is the effective cross-section. Alternatively, an unknown resistivity may be calculated by rearranging the equation as $\rho = RA/L$. The resistivity will often change with temperature. In these cases, the relevant resistivity may be calculated $\rho = \rho_{ref}(1 + \alpha(T - T_{ref}))$, where α is the resistivity proportionality constant and T is the material temperature.

Capacitors and dielectrics

Capacitors are devices used in circuits to store energy in the form of electric fields. They are most often composed of two oppositely charged parallel plates separated by a medium, generally air. This medium is referred to as the capacitor's dielectric. The dielectric material dictates the amount of energy in the electric field and, consequently, the amount of energy that can be stored by the capacitor. The measurable quality of a capacitor is known as its capacitance, or the amount of charge that it can store per volt of potential difference. This is given by the equation $C = Q/V$, with capacitance having units of farads or coulombs per volt. Physically, the capacitance depends on three things: the area of the parallel plates, the separation distance between them, and the dielectric material. For cases where the separation distance is insignificant compared to the area, the capacitance can be found by the equation $C = \varepsilon A/d$, where ε is the permittivity of the dielectric material. Often, instead of being given the permittivity, we will be given the dielectric constant, κ, which is the ratio of the permittivities of the material and air, $\kappa = \varepsilon/\varepsilon_{air}$. This yields an obvious result of $\kappa_{air} = 1$.

The energy stored in a capacitor can be calculated in three different ways: $E = CV^2/2 = Q^2/2C = VQ/2$. Another quantity associated with capacitors is the electric field energy density, η. This energy density is found by $\eta = \varepsilon E^2/2$.

Capacitors and inductors in AC circuits

Because of the constantly fluctuating nature of alternating current, capacitors and inductors both oppose immediate acceptance of the fluctuation. This opposition is referred to as impedance and is similar to resistance, also having units of ohms, but unlike resistance, impedance is a complex value, meaning that it may have an imaginary component as well as a real component. For ideal capacitors and inductors, impedance is purely imaginary, and for ideal resistors, impedance is purely real. It is only when combining the effects of these devices that the full expression for impedance, Z, is necessary: $Z = R + Xi$, where $i = \text{sqrt}(-1)$. X is a quantity known as reactance. For capacitors, $X_C = 1/\omega C$, where ω is the angular frequency of the current, and for inductors, $X_L = \omega L$.

Energy and power in electric circuits

Electric circuits operate by transferring electrical energy from one location in the circuit to another. Some devices in a circuit can store and release energy while other devices, like resistors, simply dissipate energy. Power is a measure of the rate at which energy is stored, released, transferred, or dissipated. It is measured in watts (W), or joules per second. Power is calculated by $P = VI$. The amount of power being released by a 9-V battery producing a current of 5 A is 45 W. When calculating the amount of power dissipated by a resistor, Ohm's Law allows two other equations for power, $P = I^2R = V^2/R$.

When power consumption over long periods of time needs to be measured, it will often be measured in units of kilowatt-hours, which is the amount of energy consumed at a rate of 1 kW over the course of an hour. One kilowatt-hour is equal to 3600 kJ.

Ohm's Law and Kirchoff's laws in circuit analysis

Circuit analysis is the process of determining the current or voltage drop across devices of interest in a circuit. Ohm's Law is useful in doing this since it definitively relates the current to the voltage drop for resistors, $V = IR$. Kirchoff's voltage law (KVL) states that if you sum the voltage drops across all devices in any closed loop of a circuit, the sum will always be zero, $V_1 + V_2 + \ldots + V_n = 0$. This law is particularly useful if there are multiple closed-loop pathways in a circuit. Kirchoff's current law (KCL) states that the amount of current entering a point must equal the amount of current leaving, $I_{in} = I_{out}$. This law may also be expanded to apply to the current entering and leaving a larger region of a circuit. In any given circuit analysis, it may be necessary to use all three of these laws.

Another important principle to remember in an ideal circuit is that any two points connected by only wire are at equal voltage. Only devices on the circuit may change the voltage. In actual practice, however, all wire has some amount of resistance. A battery that provides an EMF of V_B is only able to deliver a voltage to the circuit of $V = V_B - IR_B$, where R_B is the internal resistance of the battery. To express this concept in an ideal circuit, we would need to add a small resistor in series after the battery.

Circuit analysis of devices arranged in series and in parallel

When resistors in a simple circuit are arranged in series with a battery, current must pass through each resistor consecutively in order to return to the battery. This immediately tells us that the current through each resistor is the same. By KVL, we know that the sum of the voltage drop across the resistors is equal to the voltage input by the battery, $V_B = IR_1 + IR_2 + ... + IR_n$. This may be restated as $V_B = I(R_1 + R_2 + ... + R_n)$. From this we can see that for resistors arranged in series, the equivalent resistance is the sum of the resistances, $R_{eq} = R_1 + R_2 + ... + R_n$.

When resistors in a simple circuit are arranged in parallel with a battery, the current need only pass through one of them to return to the battery. By KVL, we know that the voltage drop across each resistor is the same. Since the total current must equal the sum of the currents through the resistors, we may conclude from Ohm's Law that $I = V_B/R_1 + V_B/R_2 + ... + V_B/R_n$. We may restate this relation as $I = V_B(1/R_1 + 1/R_2 + ... + 1/R_n)$. Moving the resistance expression to the other side of the equation shows us that the equivalent resistance is $R_{eq} = (1/R_1 + 1/R_2 + ... + 1/R_n)^{-1}$ for resistors in parallel.

Capacitors have opposite combination rules. Capacitors in series have an equivalent value of $C_{eq} = (1/C_1 + 1/C_2 + ... + 1/C_n)^{-1}$, while capacitors in parallel have equivalence of $C_{eq} = C_1 + C_2 + ... + C_n$.

Inductors follow the same rules as resistors.

RC circuits

An RC circuit consists of a battery wired in series with a resistor and a capacitor. Since a capacitor in steady state allows no current flow, it makes no sense to analyze a steady-state RC circuit. Instead, we will look at an RC circuit that has only just been connected, with the capacitor uncharged. The battery supplies voltage V_B to the circuit, and since the capacitor's voltage is initially zero, the voltage across the resistor is initially V_B, giving an initial current of $I = V_B/R$. As current flows, the charge on the capacitor increases, which in turn creates an opposing voltage that lowers the voltage drop across the resistor. Combining Ohm's Law with the KVL gives the voltage relation as $V_B = IR + Q/C$, where Q is the charge on the capacitor. Since the current is simply the transfer rate of the charge, this becomes a differential equation. Solving for charge and current yields the expressions $Q(t) = CV_B(1 - e^{-t/RC})$ and $I(t) = (V_B/R)e^{-t/RC}$. The factor RC in the exponential is referred to as the circuit's time constant. It is the amount of time required for the capacitor to charge up to 63.2% capacity.

If the battery is removed from the circuit after the capacitor is charged and the circuit is reconnected with just the resistor and capacitor, the capacitor will begin to drain at the same rate that it was charged. The current magnitude will follow the same equation as before, though it will be in the opposite direction. The new expression for the charge will be $Q(t) = CV_Be^{-t/RC}$.

AC circuits

Unlike DC circuits, the power provided by an AC voltage source is not constant over time. Generally, an AC source will provide voltage in a sinusoidal pattern, $V(t) = V_{max}\sin(\omega t)$. Similarly, the current will be given by $I(t) = I_{max}\sin(\omega t)$. From our known equations for power, this yields a power of $P(t) = RI_{max}^2\sin^2(\omega t)$. However, if we wish to find the average power or the amount of energy transmission after a given period of time, we need to find some way to average voltage and current. The root-mean-square (rms) method, as the name suggests, takes the square root of the time average of the squared value. For sinusoidal functions such as the voltage and current here, the rms value is the maximum value divided by the square root of 2. For voltage and current, $V_{rms} = V_{max}/\text{sqrt}(2)$, and $I_{rms} = I_{max}/\text{sqrt}(2)$. In this way, the average power can be found as $P_{av} = V_{rms}I_{rms}$, which can also be stated $P_{av} = V_{max}I_{max}/2$. A DC source with supplied voltage V_B will provide the same power over time as an AC source if $V_B = V_{rms}$.

Measuring voltage, current, resistance, and capacitance

There are several devices that allow these circuit quantities to be measured to a great degree of accuracy. An ammeter is a device placed in series with a circuit to measure the current through that location. Ideally, an ammeter has as little internal resistance as possible to prevent altering the current it is trying to measure. A voltmeter measures the voltage or potential difference between two locations in a circuit. It has two leads that are connected in parallel with the circuit and consists of a very high resistance and an ammeter in series. This allows only a very small amount of current to be diverted through the voltmeter, but enough to determine the voltage by Ohm's Law. A galvanometer is the primary working component of an ammeter. It operates based on the idea that a wire in a magnetic field will experience a force proportional to the amount of current it is carrying. It converts the observed current into a dial reading. A potentiometer is a variable resistor, often controlled by a knob, that allows an operator to control the amount of voltage or current provided to a given circuit. They are commonly used in volume-control knobs. Potentiometers can also be called voltage dividers. Their use in circuit measurement is for finding voltages by comparing them to known voltages. A multimeter is a device that combines the functions of all the above devices into one. In addition to voltage, current, resistance and capacitance, they can typically measure inductance, frequency, and other quantities.

Magnetism and magnetic field

Magnetism and magnetic attraction are similar in many ways to electrical charge and electrostatic force. Magnets have two distinct polarities, of which like polarities repel and opposite polarities attract. Just as an object that holds an electric charge will produce a vector field, so will a charged magnet. Like the electric field lines, magnetic field lines are drawn as originating from north poles and terminating on south poles. Magnetic field is typically represented with the letter **B**, and has SI units of teslas (T), which are equivalent to N/A-m. Unlike electric charge, however, an isolated magnetic pole cannot exist. Magnets must exist as dipoles, meaning that if there is a north pole, the other end of the magnet, no matter how small, will be a south pole. Most common magnets can be demagnetized simply by heating the material or subjecting it to repeated impact. This is because magnets are composed of many tiny dipoles that, when aligned, create a large unified magnet. Some materials are permanently aligned in the manner and are known as permanent magnets. Ferromagnets are iron-based materials that can be magnetized if their dipoles are aligned by a sufficiently strong magnetic field.Magnetic and electric fields are quite interrelated. It is believed that magnetic fields are set up by electric currents, and it has also been observed that magnetic fields can induce electric current. If we were to place a moving charge or a wire carrying current into a magnetic field, a magnetic force would act on it.

Forces exerted by a magnetic field on moving charged particles

We will define **B**, the magnetic field, by measuring the magnetic force exerted on a moving electric charge within the field. This is generally done by firing a test charge into the area where B is to be defined. After a time, we will find that force F_B acting on a test charge of velocity **v** and charge q can be written $F_B = q\mathbf{v}\times\mathbf{B}$, in which q can be either positive or negative. If q is negative, the direction of the force will be opposite to that shown by the right-hand rule from this cross product. From this equation, we will discover that the magnetic force always acts perpendicular to the velocity vector. This means a magnetic field can neither speed up nor slow down a charged particle; it can only deflect it. Also, a magnetic field will exert no force on a stationary charge or a charge that moves parallel to the field. We can see from this equation that the magnitude of the deflecting force will be $F_B = qvB\sin(\varphi)$, where φ is the angle between the particle velocity vector and the magnetic field vector.

Lorentz force law

The Lorentz force law describes the force exerted on a charged particle in an electromagnetic field. The force exerted on the particle with charge q can be found $F = q(\mathbf{E} + \mathbf{v}\times\mathbf{B})$, where **v** is the particle's velocity vector and **E** and **B** are the electric and magnetic field vectors, respectively. Essentially, this law states that a positively charged particle will be accelerated in the same linear direction as the electric field, but will curve perpendicularly to the magnetic field according to the right-hand rule. The Lorentz force law is used in a number of devices currently employed by physicists, like the cyclotron, magnetron, mass spectrometer, motor, generator, and rail gun.

Cyclotrons and mass spectrometers

Cyclotrons are particle accelerators that operate by using a magnetic field to create a deflection force on a fast-moving charged particle. The field strength is designed to cause the particle to move in a circular pattern. An electric field provides a force for the particle to accelerate tangentially as well. Once the particle has achieved sufficient velocity, it will exit the magnetic field and continue on in a straight line. One big advantage of the cyclotron over other types of particle accelerators is its relatively small size. Particles can achieve incredible velocities without having to travel a great distance.

Mass spectrometers are used to find the charge-to-mass ratio of ionized materials. An ionized particle of known mass, but unknown charge, is sent at a known velocity into a perpendicular magnetic field of known magnitude. Since the magnetic field is perpendicular, the tangential speed of the particle is constant. The force on a particle with constant tangential speed is equal to mv^2/r, where r is the radius of curvature of the particle's path. The force exerted by the magnetic field can be calculated as qvB, since it is perpendicular to the particle's direction of motion. Equating these two expressions gives us $q/m = v/rB$, allowing us to find the charge-to-mass ratio if we measure the radius of curvature.

Magnetic force on a straight length of current-carrying wire

A magnetic field will exert a sideways force on the conduction electrons in a wire. Since the conduction electrons cannot escape sideways out of the wire, we know that this force must be transmitted bodily to the wire itself. For instance, if we have a wire carrying current I, and we know that the longitudinal axis of the wire is perpendicular to a magnetic field **B**, then we know that a force equal to $(-e)vB$ will act on each conduction electron. Taken as a whole, the wire will experience a force of ILB, where L is the length of wire in the field. If we were to reverse either the magnetic field or the direction of the current, then the force on the wire would reverse as well. If the magnetic field is not perpendicular to the wire, then we can find the magnetic force as F_B = ILBsin(φ), where φ is the angle between the direction of current and the magnetic field vector.

The torque on a current-carrying loop is a result of the same phenomenon, except that with a loop, the current travels in opposite directions on opposite sides of the loop. This causes a result of zero net force since all the current exits the field from the same direction that it entered. There is, however, a net torque since the current going in opposite directions is separated by a distance. The torque can be found by τ = IA**n**×**B**, where A is the area enclosed by the loop and **n** is the unit vector perpendicular to the plane of the loop. The loop may be any shape so long as it does not cross itself and is a closed shape.

Gauss's law for magnetism

Gauss's law for magnetism solidifies the assertion that magnetic monopoles cannot exist. It does so by making statements about magnetic flux, which is defined in much the same way as electric flux, Φ_m = **B·A**, where **A** is the surface's normal vector. Magnetic flux has SI units of webers (Wb). If the surface is taken to be an enclosing surface, or a Gaussian surface, Gauss's law states that the total flux through the surface will equal zero. Unlike the case with electric flux, which allows for contained net charge, there can be no net magnetic poles inside of a closed surface. For every north pole, there must be a south pole of equal magnitude. If, for instance, we envision our Gaussian surface as enclosing one end of a short solenoid (which will set up a magnetic field resembling that of a magnetic dipole), we will notice that the magnetic field *B* will enter the Gaussian surface inside the solenoid (at the north pole) and will leave it outside the solenoid. No lines will begin or end in the interior of the surface, so the total flux for the surface is zero.

Biot-Savart law and Ampere's law

Any current-carrying wire will produce a magnetic field that circles the wire in the direction indicated by the right-hand rule (with the thumb pointing in the direction of the current). The Biot-Savart law gives the magnitude and direction of the magnetic field created by each infinitesimal element of current. The equation form of this law is given as **dB** = (μ_0I/4r^3pi)***dL×r**, where μ_0 is a physical constant called the permeability of free space, **dL** is an infinitesimal vector pointing along the length of the wire in the direction of current, and **r** is the vector pointing from the wire element to the location where the field is to be calculated. Integrating this expression along the full length of wire gives the total resultant field. Ampere's law states this concept in the form of a closed-loop line integral:

$$\oint_C B \cdot dL = \mu_0 I$$

For transient cases, such as RC circuits, it is necessary to take into account what is known as the displacement current. Displacement current is found by the equation $I_d = \varepsilon_0(\partial\Phi_e/\partial t)$, where ε_0 is the permittivity of free space and ∂Φe/∂t is the instantaneous rate of change of electric flux. It is not actually a current, but for use in Ampere's law, it is treated like one. Thus, for transient cases, the I in Ampere's law is calculated as $I = I_{actual} + I_d$.

Application of Ampere's law to a straight wire, a loop of wire, and a solenoid

Ampere's law is described by the closed-loop line integral:

$$\oint_C B \cdot dL = \mu_0 I$$

For a straight length of wire, the magnetic field simply encircles the wire in the direction indicated by the right-hand rule (with the thumb pointed in the direction of current and the fingers curling to indicate the magnetic field). For a very long wire where end effects may be ignored, the magnetic field is given as $B = \mu_0 I/(2pi*r)$, where r is the distance from the wire.

For a loop of current-carrying wire, the magnetic field direction can still be determined from the right-hand rule. However, the field magnitude at most points around and inside the loop is difficult to determine. The field magnitude at the center of the loop is found to be $B = \mu_0 I/2r$.

For a solenoid, a long coil of current-carrying wire that is sometimes wrapped around a metal core, the magnetic field direction may again be determined by the right-hand rule. At all points inside the solenoid, the field has magnitude $B = \mu_0 nI/h$, where n is the number of loops in the solenoid and h is its height. For a long solenoid, it can be shown that the field magnitude outside the solenoid is negligible.

Electromagnetic induction

Electromagnetic induction is the process by which current is induced due to a change in magnetic flux. One or more loops of wire in a magnetic field have magnetic flux through them of $\Phi_m = BA\cos(\theta)$, where A is the area enclosed by the loop and θ is the angle between a vector normal to the plane of the loop and the magnetic field vector. The produced EMF can be found by Faraday's law, stated in equation form as $V_{emf} = -N(d\Phi_m/dt)$, where N is the number of loops in the coil. So, this induced voltage will exist only as long as Φ_m is changing. A change in any of the variables (B, A, or θ) can cause a change in magnetic flux. Generators operate by rotating a coil in a constant magnetic field.

The contribution to this concept by Lenz's law is the negative sign in the equation of Faraday's law. Lenz's law states that the induced emf will try to counter the changing magnetic flux by creating a current to produce another magnetic field opposing the change in magnetic flux.

Transformers, generators, and electric motors

Transformers are devices that allow power to be exchanged between two circuits through electromagnetic induction. They generally consist of a pair of coils wrapped around a single metal core. The magnetic field induced by the current in one coil in turn induces a current in the second coil. The amount of current induced in the second coil is dependent on the inducing current and the number of loops in each coil: $I_2/I_1 = N_1/N_2$, where N is the number of loops in the given coil. Since the power given up by the one circuit is the same as that received by the second circuit, we may also say that $V_1I_1 = V_2I_2$, or equivalently $I_2/I_1 = V_1/V_2$.

Generators operate by using mechanical energy to turn a coil in a magnetic field, thus converting it to electrical energy. Often, large generators will require gasoline combustion engines to provide the necessary power to operate, though some are able to tap natural power sources such as flowing water. Smaller generators may be powered by hand cranks or stationary bicycles.

Electric motors are basically the reverse of generators. They operate by using an alternating current source connected to an electromagnet to create an oscilating magnetic field that causes a current-carrying coil to rotate, thus generating a torque. DC motors require additional parts to direct the flow of current in such a way that the coil will be continuously rotating.

Velocity, amplitude, wavelength, and frequency

The velocity of a wave is the rate at which it travels in a given medium. It is defined in the same way that velocity of physical objects is defined, a change in position divided by a change in time. A single wave may have a different velocity for every medium in which it travels. Some types of waves, such as light waves, do not require a medium.

Amplitude is one measure of a wave's strength. It is half the verticle distance between the highest and lowest points on the wave, the crest and trough, respectively. The vertical midpoint, halfway between the crest and trough, is sometimes called an equilibrium point, or a node. Amplitude is often denoted with an A.

The wavelength is the horizontal distance between successive crests or troughs, or the distance between the first and third of three successive nodes. Wavelength is generally denoted as λ.

Frequency is the number of crests or troughs that pass a particular point in a given period of time. It is the inverse of the period, the time required for the wave to cycle from one crest or trough to the next. Frequency, f, is generally measured in hertz, or cycles per second.

Velocity, wavelength, and frequency are not independent quantities. They are related by the expression $v = \lambda f$.

Intensity

Intensity is a physical quantity, equivalent to the flux through a given area over a period of time. It may also be defined as the energy density of a wave times its velocity. Intensity has units of watts per square meter. The intensity of light decreases as the distance from the light source increases. The inverse square law states that the intensity is inversely proportional to the square of the distance from the source. It is also directly proportional to the power of the light source. This is shown mathematically by the expression $I = CP/r^2$, where C is the proportionality constant. This may be better understood by imagining the light waves emanating from a source as an expanding sphere. As their distance from the source increases as r, the area over which they must divide themselves increases as $4pi*r^2$.

Interaction of light waves with matter

When light waves make contact with matter, they are either reflected, transmitted, or absorbed. If the light is reflected from the surface of the matter, the angle at which it hits the surface will be the same as the angle at which it leaves. If the ray of light is perpendicular to the surface, it will be reflected back in the direction from which it came.

When light is transmitted from one medium to another, its direction may be altered upon entering the new medium. This is known as refraction. The degree to which the light is refracted depends on the speed at which light travels in each medium.

Light that is neither reflected nor transmitted will be absorbed by the surface and stored as heat energy. Because there are no ideal surfaces, most light and matter interaction will be a combination of two or even all three of these. Another result of imperfect surfaces is scattering, which occurs when waves are reflected in multiple directions. Rayleigh scattering is the specific case of a light wave being scattered by tiny particles that single out particular wavelengths. Dust particles in the atmosphere scatter primarily the blue wavelength of sunlight to give our sky a predominantly blue hue.

Transverse and longitudinal waves

Transverse waves are waves whose oscillations are perpendicular to the direction of motion. A light wave is an example of a transverse wave. A group of light waves traveling in the same direction will be oscillating in several different planes. Light waves are said to be polarized when they are filtered such that only waves oscillating in a particular plane are allowed to pass, with the remainder being absorbed by the filter. If two such polarizing filters are employed successively and aligned to allow different planes of oscillation, they will block all light waves.

Longitudinal waves are waves that oscillate in the same direction as their primary motion. Their motion is restricted to a single axis, so they may not be polarized. A sound wave is an example of a longitudinal wave.

Doppler effect

One common phenomenon of wave motion is the Doppler effect. It is a disparity between the emitted frequency and the observed frequency. It is the caused by relative motion between the wave source and the observer. If the source and observer are both moving toward one another, the observed frequency is determined by the following equation: $f_o = f_e(v_W + v_o)/(v_W - v_S)$, where v_W is the speed of the wave. If the source or the observer is moving in the opposite direction, its sign must be reversed. The Doppler effect is most commonly observed when sound waves change pitch as an observer's relative motion to a train or emergency vehicle changes. The Doppler effect is also employed in the operation of speed-detecting radar guns. Microwaves are emitted at a known frequency and, after being reflected by the object in question, return at a different frequency, giving the object's speed.

Resonance and natural frequency

Every physical object has one or more natural frequencies, or frequencies at which it will naturally vibrate. The natural frequency is based on the object's dimensions, density, orientation, and other factors. If the object is acted on by a periodic force, it will vibrate at its natural frequency, regardless of the forcing frequency. If the excitation force is operating at the object's natural frequency, the object will experience resonance, in which the object receives all of the energy exerted by the excitation force. The amplitude of the vibration will increase rapidly and without bound until either the excitation force changes frequency or the natural frequency of the object is altered.

Sound waves

The pitch of a sound as it reaches one's ear is based on the frequency of the sound waves. A high-pitched sound has a higher frequency than a low-pitched sound. Like all waves, sound waves transmit energy. The rate at which this energy is transmitted is the sonic power. Loudness, or intensity of sound, is the sonic power received per unit area.

Beats occur when a pair of sound waves, whose frequencies differ only slightly, interfere with one another. This interference causes a periodic variation in sound intensity, whose frequency is equal to the difference between that of the two sound waves. This is noticeable when tuning two instruments to one another. As the two pitches get closer, the beat frequency will become smaller and smaller until it disappears entirely, indicating that the instruments are in tune.

Standing waves

A standing wave is the result of interference between two waves of the same frequency moving in opposite directions. These waves, although in constant motion, have certain points on the wave where the amplitude is zero, locations referred to as nodes. One example of a standing wave is a plucked guitar string. Since the string is attached at both ends, the fixed ends will be nodes. The primary tone will be that of the fundamental, or first harmonic, shown in the first figure below. It has a wavelength of twice the length of the string, L. The other three pictures below are those of the second through fourth harmonics. The nth harmonic has wavelength and frequency of $\lambda_n = 2L/n$ and $f_n = nv/2L$, where v is wave velocity.

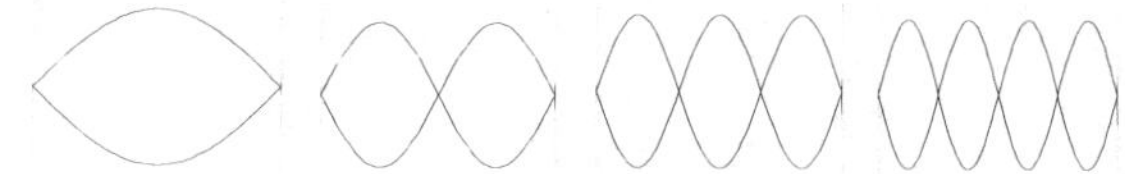

This same phenomenon occurs inside the tubes of wind instruments, though it is much more difficult to visualize. With a tube, however, there will be one or two open ends. Rather than a node, each open end will coincide with an antinode: that is, a crest or trough. For waves in a tube with two open ends, the wavelength and frequency calculations are the same as those for the plucked string. For the case with one open end, only the odd harmonics will be seen. The frequency of the nth harmonic becomes $f_n = nv/4L$, where n is odd.

Electromagnetic spectrum

The electromagnetic spectrum is the range of all wavelengths and frequencies of known electromagnetic waves. Visible light occupies only a small portion of the electromagnetic spectrum. Some of the common classifications of electromagnetic waves are listed in the table below with their approximate frequency ranges.

Classification	Freq. (Hz)
Gamma Rays	$\sim 10^{19}$
X-Rays	$\sim 10^{17} - 10^{18}$
Ultraviolet	$\sim 10^{15} - 10^{16}$
Visible Light	$\sim 10^{14}$
Infra-red	$\sim 10^{11} - 10^{14}$
Microwaves	$\sim 10^{10} - 10^{11}$
Radio/TV	$\sim 10^{6} - 10^{9}$

Electromagnetic waves travel at the speed of light, $c = 3 \times 10^8$ m/s. To find the wavelength of any electromagnetic wave, simply divide c by the frequency. Visible light occupies a range of wavelengths from approximately 380 nm (violet) to 740 nm (red). The full spectrum of color can be found between these two wavelengths.

Wave superposition and interference

The principle of linear superposition states that two or more waves occupying the same space create an effect equal to the sum of their individual amplitudes at that location. This is known as interference. If the resultant amplitude is larger than either individual amplitude, it is constructive interference. Similarly, if the interference reduces the effect, it is considered destructive.

Some special cases of interference are standing waves and beats, in which two waves having the same and nearly the same frequency, respectively, interfere with one another. Another concept related to interference is phase. If two waves with the same frequency are in phase, then they have perfectly constructive interference. The nodes in each wave will line up, as will the respective crests and troughs. If those same two waves are 180 degrees out of phase, they will experience perfectly destructive interference. The nodes will still line up, but each crest will be aligned with a trough, and vice versa. From this it can be seen that constructive interference results in a larger wave amplitude than destructive interference. If two identical waves are 180 degrees out of phase, the resultant wave will have zero amplitude. This effect is the design impetus for some noise-cancellation technology.

Young's double-slit experiment and thin-film interference

Thomas Young's double-slit experiment visually demonstrated the interference between two sets of light waves. It consisted of shining light through two thin, closely spaced parallel slits and onto a screen. The interference between light waves from the two slits caused a pattern of alternately light and dark bands to appear on the screen, due to constructive and destructive interference, respectively. The dimensions of the experimental setup can be used to determine the wavelength of the light being projected onto the screen. This is given by the equation $\lambda = yd/x$, where y is the distance between the centers of two light bands, d is the distance between the slits, and x is the distance from the slits to the screen. Thin-film interference is caused when incident light is reflected both by a partially reflective thin layer on a surface and by the surface itself. This interference may be constructive or destructive.

Diffraction and dispersion

Diffraction occurs when a wave encounters a physical object. It includes phenomena such as bending, diverging, and other aperture effects. When light emerges from a single small slit, a rippling effect may be observed. The results of Young's double-slit experiment are due to diffraction as the light waves from these slits diverge. Similarly, light emerging from a circular aperture will project concentric light and dark rings due to diffraction. Diffraction grating is an arrangement of material whose reflective properties are intentionally varied at equally spaced intervals. Due to the arrangement, incident light is reflected in specific directions, known as diffraction orders, based on its wavelength.

Dispersion occurs when light consisting of multiple wavelengths enters a medium whose propagation behavior depends on the wavelength of transmitted light. This is what is observed when light passes through a prism, splitting it into its component colors.

Geometry of refraction and reflection

When light is transmitted from one medium to another, its direction may be altered upon entering the new medium. This is known as refraction. The degree to which the light is refracted depends on the index of refraction, n, for each medium. The index of refraction is a ratio of the speed of light in a vacuum to the speed of light in the medium in question, $n = c/v_m$. Since light can never travel faster than it does in a vacuum, the index of refraction is always greater than one. Snell's law gives the equation for determining the angle of refraction: $n_1\sin(\theta_1) = n_2\sin(\theta_2)$, where n is the index of refraction for each medium, and θ is the angle the light makes with the normal vector on each side of the interface between the two media.

We will examine a special case by trying to determine the angle of refraction for light traveling from a medium with $n_1 = 3$ to another medium with $n_2 = 1.5$. The light makes an angle $\theta_1 = 35°$ with the normal. Using Snell's law, we find that $\sin(\theta_2) = 1.15$. Since this is not mathematically possible, we conclude that the light cannot be refracted. This case is known as total internal reflection. When light travels from a more dense medium to a less dense medium, there is a minimum angle of incidence, beyond which all light will be reflected. This critical angle is $\theta_1 = \sin^{-1}(n_2/n_1)$. Fiber-optic cables make use of this phenomenon to ensure that the signal is fully reflected internally when it veers into the outer walls of the fiber.

Thin lenses

A lens is an optical device that redirects light to either converge or diverge in specific geometric patterns. Whether the lens converges or diverges is dependent on the lens being convex or concave, respectively. The particular angle of redirection is dictated by the lens's focal length. For a converging lens, this is the distance from the lens that parallel rays entering from the opposite side would intersect. For a diverging lens, it is the distance from the lens that parallel rays entering the lens would intersect if they were reverse extrapolated. However, the focal length of a diverging lens is always considered to be negative. A thin lens is a lens whose focal length is much greater than its thickness. By making this assumption, we can derive many helpful relations.

Images

In optics, an object's image is what is seen when the object is viewed through a lens. The location of an object's image is related to the lens's focal length by the equation $1/d_o + 1/d_i = 1/f$, where f is the focal length, and d_o and d_i are the distance of the object and its image from the lens, respectively. A positive d_i indicates that the image is on the opposite side of the lens from the object. If the lens is a magnifying lens, the height of the object may be different from that of its image, and may even be inverted. The object's magnification, m, can be found as $m = -d_i/d_o$. The value for the magnification can then be used to relate the object's height to that of its image: $m = y_i/y_o$. Note that if the magnification is negative, then the image has been inverted.

Images may be either real or virtual. Real images are formed by light rays passing through the image location, while virtual images are only perceived by reverse extrapolating refracted light rays. Diverging lenses cannot create real images, only virtual ones. Real images are always on the opposite side of a converging lens from the object and are always inverted.

Plane mirrors and spherical mirrors

Plane mirrors have very simple properties. They reflect only virtual images, they have no magnification, and the object's distance from the mirror is always equal to that of its image. Plane mirrors will also appear to reverse the directions left and right.

Spherical mirrors follow the same governing equations for finding image height, location, orientation, and magnification as do thin lenses; however, the sign convention for image location is reversed. A positive image location denotes that it is on the same side as the object. Spherical mirrors may be either concave or convex. Convex mirrors are by far the simpler of the two. They will always reflect virtual, upright images with magnification between zero and one. Concave mirrors have varying behavior based on the object location.

Concave mirrors

Concave mirrors will create an image of an object in varying ways depending on the location of the object. The table below details the location, orientation, magnification, and nature of the image. The five object locations to be examined are between the mirror and the focal point (1), at the focal point (2), between the focal point and the center of curvature, or twice the focal point (3), at the center of curvature (4), and beyond the center of curvature (5).

	Location	Orientation	Magnification	Nature
1	$d_i < 0$	upright	$m > 1$	virtual
2	none	none	none	none
3	$d_i > 2f$	inverted	$m < -1$	real
4	$d_i = 2f$	inverted	$m = -1$	real
5	$f < d_i < 2f$	inverted	$0 > m > -1$	real

Note in case 5 that the image may effectively be located at the focal point. This is the case for objects at extremely great, or near infinite, distances from the mirror. The magnification at these distances will be very small and a true infinite distance would result in a magnification of zero.

Prisms

Prisms are optical devices that alter the path or nature of light waves. Glass and plastic are the two most prevalent materials used to make prisms. There are three different types of prisms in common use. The most familiar of these is the dispersive prism, which splits a beam of light into its constituent wavelengths. For sunlight, this results in the full spectrum of color being displayed. These prisms are generally in the familiar triangular prism shape.

Polarizing prisms, as their name suggests, polarize light, but without significantly reducing the intensity, as a simple filter would. Waves that are oscillating in planes other than the desired plane are caused to rotate, so that they are oscillating in the desired plane. This type of prism is commonly used in cameras.

Reflective prisms are much less common than either of the others. They reflect light, often through the use of the total internal reflection phenomenon. Their primary use is in binoculars.

Optical instruments

A simple magnifier, or commonly a magnifying glass, is a converging lens that creates an enlarged virtual image near the observer's eye. The object must be within a certain distance, about 25 cm or 10 inches, from the magnifier for it to operate properly. Otherwise, the image will be blurry.

A microscope is a magnifying device that is used to examine very small objects. It uses a series of lenses to capture light coming from the far side of the sample under examination. Often microscopes will have interchangeable magnification lenses mounted on a wheel, allowing the user to adjust the level of magnification by rotating in a different lens. Optical microscopes will generally be limited to a magnification of 1500.

Telescopes are used to view very distant objects, most often celestial bodies. Telescopes use both lenses and mirrors to capture light from a distant source, focus it, and then magnify it. This creates a virtual image that is very much smaller than the object itself, and yet much larger than the object appears to the naked eye.

Practice Test

Practice Questions

1. Starting from rest, a bicyclist accelerates in one direction at a constant 2 m/s^2. What is his instantaneous speed after 10 seconds?

Ⓐ 2 m/s

Ⓑ 5 m/s

Ⓒ 20 m/s

Ⓓ 40 m/s

2. Electrical wires are often made of copper covered with rubber. Which of the following best describes the reason for this?

Ⓐ Copper and rubber are both conductors

Ⓑ Copper and rubber are both insulators

Ⓒ Copper is a conductor; rubber is an insulator

Ⓓ Copper is an insulator; rubber is a conductor

3. A merry-go-round three meters in diameter takes 20 seconds to make a full rotation with no external forces acting on it. What is the linear speed of a horse at the edge of the merry-go-round?

Ⓐ 0.15 m/s

Ⓑ 0.47 m/s

Ⓒ 0.24 m/s

Ⓓ 0.94 m/s

4. If the average speed of the molecules in a gas increases, which of the following *must* be true?

Ⓐ The temperature of the gas increases

Ⓑ The pressure of the gas increases

Ⓒ The volume of the gas increases

Ⓓ The volume of the gas decreases

5. A catapult flings a stone with an initial velocity of 10 m/s at an angle of 40° from the horizontal. Assuming that the stone lands at the same altitude as its starting point and ignoring air resistance, how far away from the catapult will the stone land? Record your answer in meters and bubble in your answer to the nearest tenth on the answer document.

Question 6 pertains to the following graph of displacement from equilibrium versus time for a point on a vibrating string:

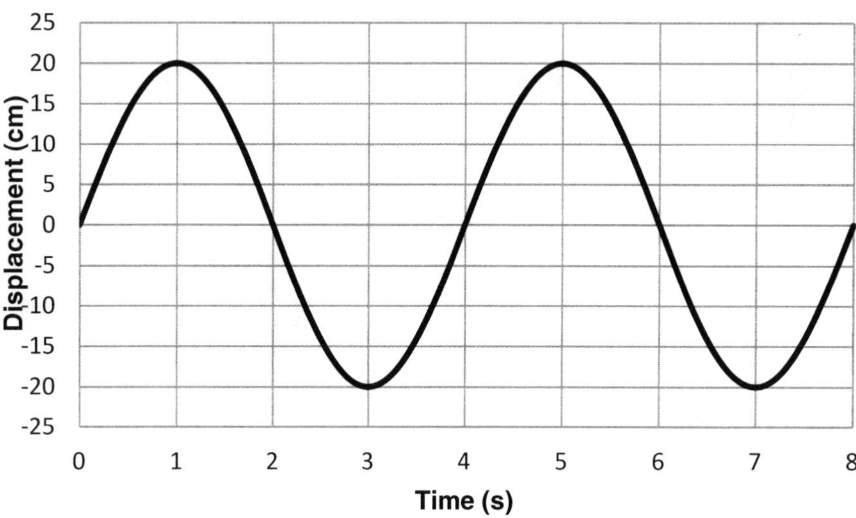

6. Which of the following characteristics of the wave *cannot* be determined from the graph?

Ⓐ Amplitude

Ⓑ Frequency

Ⓒ Period

Ⓓ Wavelength

7. A rock rests on a table. Which of the following is the reaction to the pull of the Earth's gravity on the rock?

Ⓐ The pull of the rock's gravity on the Earth

Ⓑ The pull of the Earth's gravity on the table

Ⓒ The normal force exerted on the rock by the table

Ⓓ The force of friction between the rock and the table

8. Which of the following scientists is *not* known for having played an important role in the study of electromagnetism?

Ⓐ Niels Bohr

Ⓑ Charles-Augustin de Coulomb

Ⓒ Michael Faraday

Ⓓ James Clerk Maxwell

9. A roller coaster car travels on a frictionless track along a flat section before entering a loop the top of which is ten meters higher than the flat section. What is the minimum speed at which the car must be traveling along the flat section in order to reach the top of the loop?

Ⓐ 5 m/s

Ⓑ 7 m/s

Ⓒ 10 m/s

Ⓓ 14 m/s

10. Which of the following best describes the image of a distant object as seen through a thin convex lens?

Ⓐ Real and upright

Ⓑ Real and inverted

Ⓒ Virtual and upright

Ⓓ Virtual and inverted

11. A metal block hangs from a spring. Which of the following is a correct force-body diagram for the forces acting on the block?

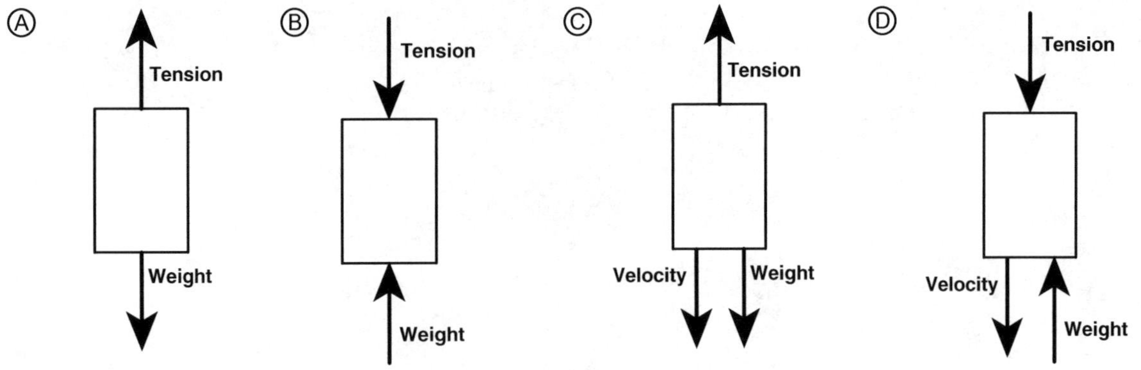

Ⓐ Tension Weight

Ⓑ Tension Weight

Ⓒ Tension Velocity Weight

Ⓓ Tension Velocity Weight

12. The mass of the planet Uranus is 8.7×10^{25} kg. The mass of the Sun is 2.0×10^{30} kg. The distance between Uranus and the Sun at one point in its orbit is about 2.9×10^{9} km. What is the magnitude of the gravitational force between the Sun and Uranus at this point?

Ⓐ 4.0×10^{36} N

Ⓑ 4.0×10^{33} N

Ⓒ 1.4×10^{27} N

Ⓓ 1.4×10^{21} N

13. A crane lifts a crate 10 meters off the ground and then lowers it onto a platform 6 meters above the ground. If the crate has a weight of 1000 N, what is the net work done by the crane?

Ⓐ 14000 J

Ⓑ 10000 J

Ⓒ 6000 J

Ⓓ 4000 J

14. The AC voltage across the wires on the left side of the transformer diagrammed here is 150 V at its peak. What is the peak voltage across the wires on the right side?

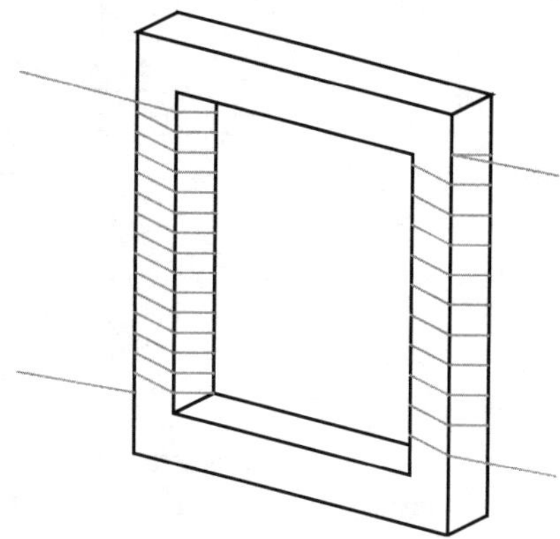

Ⓐ 15 V

Ⓑ 100 V

Ⓒ 150 V

Ⓓ 225 V

15. An elevator has a mass of 500 kg and can carry a maximum load of 1500 kg. What power is necessary to make the fully loaded elevator rise at a speed of 2.5 m/s? Record and bubble in your answer to the nearest kilowatt on the answer document.

16. **Shown below are the approximate emission spectra of some common elements.**

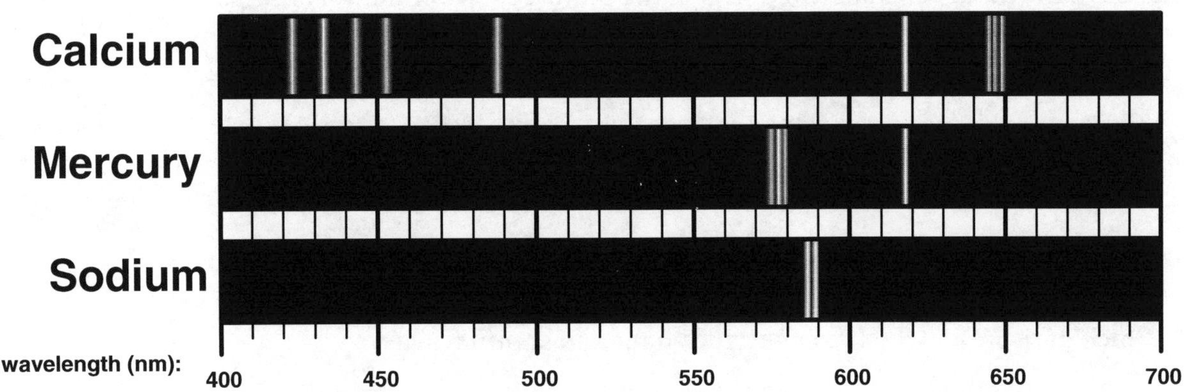

Using this information, state what elements you would expect a sample to contain that showed the following emission spectrum.

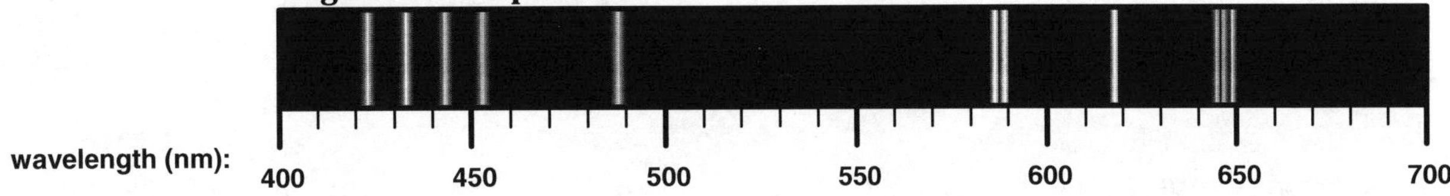

Ⓐ Calcium and mercury

Ⓑ Calcium and sodium

Ⓒ Mercury and sodium

Ⓓ Calcium, mercury, and sodium

17. **Which of the following graphs most accurately displays velocity *v* versus time *t* of a ball rolling down a constant slope?**

Ⓐ

Ⓑ

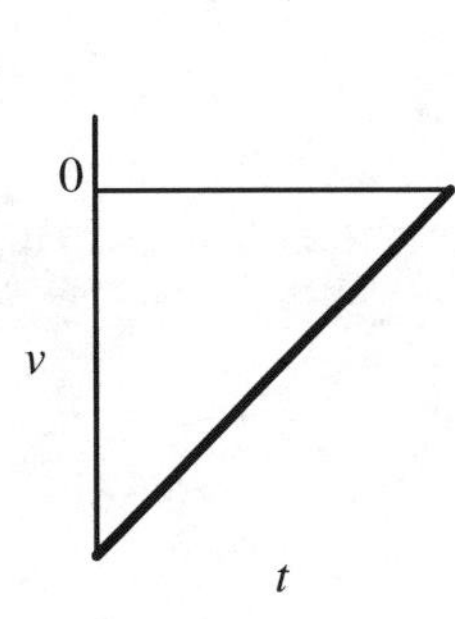

Ⓒ

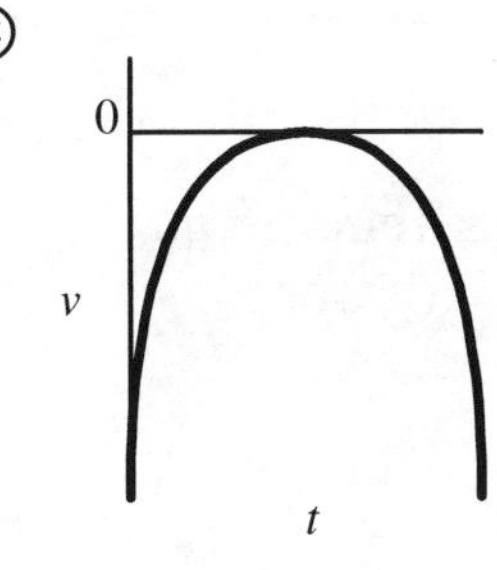

Ⓓ

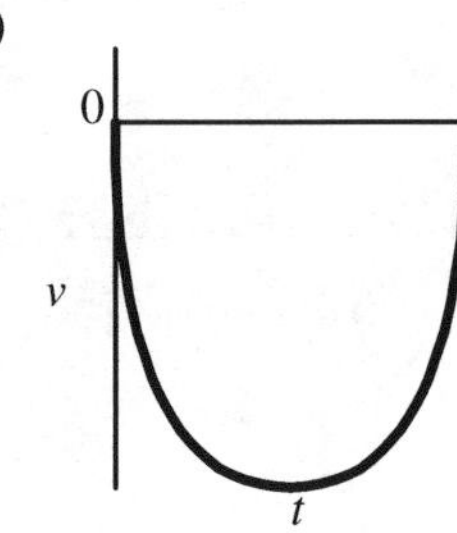

18. A soccer ball with a mass of 0.4 kg rolls toward a soccer player at a speed of 1 m/s. He kicks the ball, giving it a speed of 8 m/s in the opposite direction. What impulse did his kick produce on the soccer ball?

Ⓐ 0.4 kg m/s

Ⓑ 2.8 kg m/s

Ⓒ 3.2 kg m/s

Ⓓ 3.6 kg m/s

19. Which of the following best describes light and sound waves?

Ⓐ Light and sound are both transverse waves

Ⓑ Light and sound are both longitudinal waves

Ⓒ Light is a transverse wave; sound is a longitudinal wave

Ⓓ Light is a longitudinal wave; sound is a transverse wave

20. Three students pull ropes attached to a ring as shown in the diagram. One student pulls due south with a force of 100 N, another pulls due east with an unknown force, and the third pulls in some direction north-northwest with a force of 115 N. The ring does not move. What is the magnitude of the unknown force?

Ⓐ 15 N

Ⓑ 57 N

Ⓒ 81 N

Ⓓ 108 N

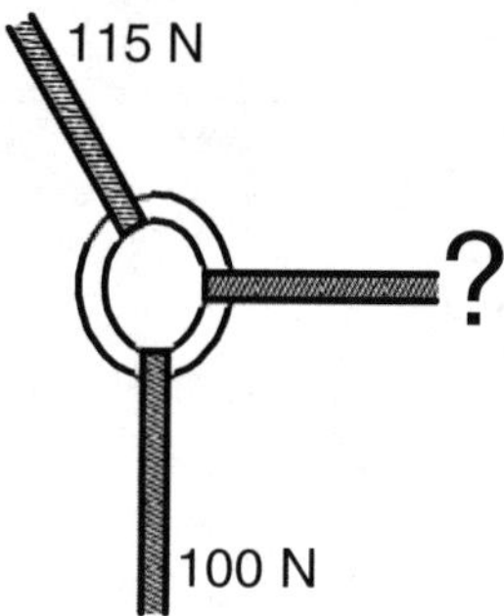

21. Which of the following items do *not* rely directly on magnetic forces to operate?

Ⓐ Cassette tapes

Ⓑ Compact discs

Ⓒ Compasses

Ⓓ Maglev trains

22. When you walk barefoot on a hot sidewalk, what process is primarily responsible for heat transfer from the sidewalk to your foot?

Ⓐ Conduction

Ⓑ Convection

Ⓒ Radiation

Ⓓ None of the above.

23. Which of the following observations provides the best evidence that sound can travel through solid objects?

Ⓐ Sound waves cannot travel through a vacuum.

Ⓑ The atoms of a solid are packed tightly together.

Ⓒ If you knock on a solid object, it makes a sound.

Ⓓ You can hear a sound on the other side of a solid wall.

24. A cannon is recessed in a pit so that the mouth of the cannon is at the same altitude as the ground. A cannonball is fired into the air and hits the ground 4 seconds later. What height did the cannonball reach at its peak?

Ⓐ 19.6 m

Ⓑ 39.2 m

Ⓒ 78.4 m

Ⓓ 156.8 m

25. The frequency of the light in a typical red He-Ne laser is 4.74×10^{14} Hz. What is its wavelength in nanometers? Record and bubble in your answer to the nearest nanometer on the answer document.

26. In the circuit pictured to the right, what is the current at point A?

Ⓐ 13.3 mA

Ⓑ 35 mA

Ⓒ 60 mA

Ⓓ 154 mA

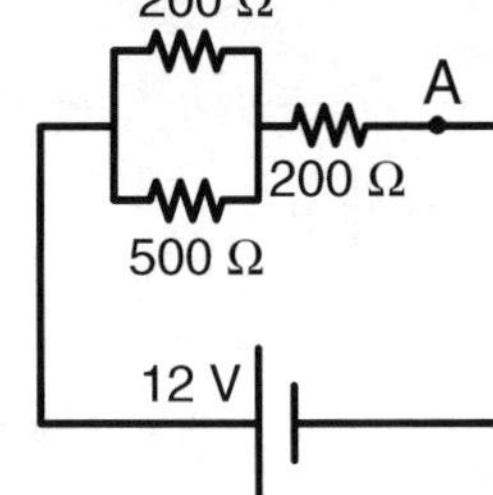

27. An inventor has an idea to create a plane that needs no fuel because it uses heat energy from the air, cooling the air to a lower temperature than anything in the plane and using the heat energy thus extracted to run the plane. Why wouldn't it actually be possible to build such a plane?

Ⓐ It violates conservation of energy

Ⓑ It violates conservation of mass

Ⓒ It violates conservation of momentum

Ⓓ It violates the law of entropy

28. Jim exerts a force of 320 N to push a heavy barrel along a floor surface with significant friction. He manages to impart to the barrel an acceleration of 0.13 m/s^2. If the barrel has a mass of 200 kg, what is the magnitude of the force of friction acting on the barrel?

Ⓐ 26 N

Ⓑ 147 N

Ⓒ 294 N

Ⓓ 320 N

29. Which of the following accurately describes an effect of the weak nuclear force?

Ⓐ It binds quarks into protons

Ⓑ It binds nucleons together into atomic nuclei

Ⓒ It binds protons to electrons to form atoms

Ⓓ It causes subatomic particles to decay

30. Two hydrogen nuclei fuse into a helium nucleus, releasing a burst of energy. If you could measure the masses before and after the nuclear reaction with an extremely sensitive scale, which of the following would you expect to find?

Ⓐ The two hydrogen nuclei have a slightly larger total mass than the helium nucleus

Ⓑ The two hydrogen nuclei have a slightly smaller total mass than the helium nucleus

Ⓒ The two hydrogen nuclei have exactly the same total mass as the helium nucleus

Ⓓ The hydrogen nuclei and the helium nucleus are all massless

31. **The mass of an electron is 9.1×10^{-31} kg. The mass of a proton is 1.6×10^{-27} kg. The charge of an electron is -1.6×10^{-19} C. What is the magnitude of the electromagnetic force between a proton and an electron that are 0.1 mm apart?**

Ⓐ 1.7×10^{-40} N

Ⓑ 1.3×10^{-39} N

Ⓒ 2.3×10^{-20} N

Ⓓ 0.14 N

32. **A submarine is cruising north, at a speed of 10 m/s relative to a nearby island. It fires a torpedo directly to its right (that is, at a right angle to its direction of motion) at a speed of 25 m/s relative to the submarine. What is the initial speed of the torpedo relative to the island?**

Ⓐ 15 m/s

Ⓑ 20 m/s

Ⓒ 27 m/s

Ⓓ 35 m/s

33. **A light ray passes from air into a block of amber as shown in this diagram. What is the index of refraction of amber?**

Ⓐ 1.11

Ⓑ 1.55

Ⓒ 1.60

Ⓓ 1.66

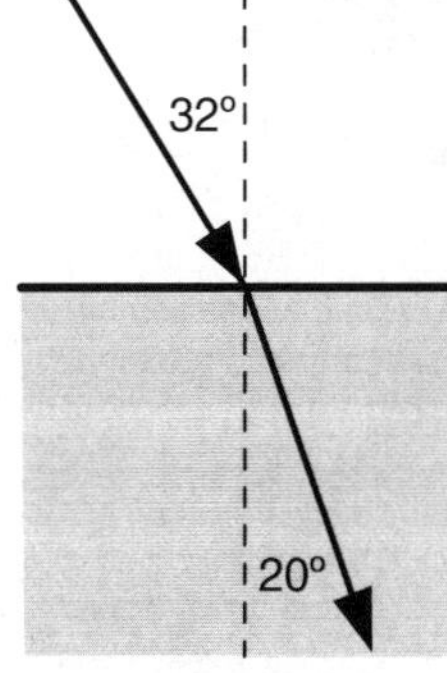

34. **A bus is moving down a street at 10 m/s. A man walks to the back of the bus at a speed of 1 m/s, dragging a suitcase. What is the speed of the suitcase?**

Ⓐ 0 m/s

Ⓑ 1 m/s

Ⓒ 9 m/s

Ⓓ It depends on the frame of reference

35. A rocket with a mass of 1000 kg is launched horizontally and propelled to a final velocity of 200 m/s. An identical rocket has a payload attached with a mass of an additional 500 kg. If both rockets have the same fuel efficiency, what will the final velocity of the second rocket be when it is launched horizontally? Record and bubble in your answer in m/s on the answer document, to the nearest tenth.

36. Which of the following best explains why medical imaging machines use x-rays instead of visible light?

Ⓐ X-rays have shorter wavelengths than visible light, which lets them penetrate matter more easily

Ⓑ X-rays have longer wavelengths than visible light, which lets them penetrate matter more easily

Ⓒ X-rays have shorter wavelengths than visible light, which means they are more energetic

Ⓓ X-rays have longer wavelengths than visible light, which means they are less energetic

37. The speed of a small wheeled robot is measured by dividing the distance between two marked points by the time the robot takes to travel between the two points. The distance is recorded as 1.000 meters, as measured by a meter stick that can measure to the nearest millimeter, and the time is recorded as 5.00 seconds, as measured with a stopwatch that can measure to the nearest 0.01 seconds. Which of the following best expresses the measurement of the robot's speed and its uncertainty?

Ⓐ 0.20000 m/s ± 0.000224 m/s

Ⓑ 0.20000 m/s ± 0.00045 m/s

Ⓒ 0.200 m/s ± 0.00045 m/s

Ⓓ 0.200 m/s ± 0.000224 m/s

38. Which two of the four fundamental forces were recognized as two manifestations of a single interaction and combined in a unified theory?

Ⓐ The strong and weak nuclear forces

Ⓑ Gravity and the strong nuclear force

Ⓒ Electromagnetism and the weak nuclear force

Ⓓ Gravity and electromagnetism

39. Which of the following correctly describes the relationship between the work done on an object and its change in kinetic energy?

Ⓐ The work done on an object is always greater than its change in kinetic energy

Ⓑ The work done on an object is always less than its change in kinetic energy

Ⓒ The work done on an object is always equal to its change in kinetic energy

Ⓓ The work done on an object may be greater than, less than, or equal to its change in kinetic energy

40. Which of the following best describes how quantum phenomena relate to the working of electron microscopes?

Ⓐ Light behaves as a particle, allowing the microscope to hit the observed object with one photon at a time

Ⓑ Electrons behave as waves, allowing beams of electrons to be diffracted by and reflect from and thereby "illuminate" objects

Ⓒ The uncertainty principle allows the microscope to determine an object's exact contours

Ⓓ Quantum entanglement ensures that the observed object is "entangled" with the observer

41. A scientist mixes two chemicals together, and they produce a violent reaction, generating considerable heat. Where did the thermal energy come from to heat up the chemicals?

Ⓐ The kinetic energy of the molecules in the chemicals

Ⓑ Potential energy inherent in the atomic bonds in the molecules of the chemicals

Ⓒ It was absorbed from the surrounding air

Ⓓ Nowhere; the energy was completely created by the reaction

42. Four synchronized photogates are set up on an inclined track as shown in the diagram below.

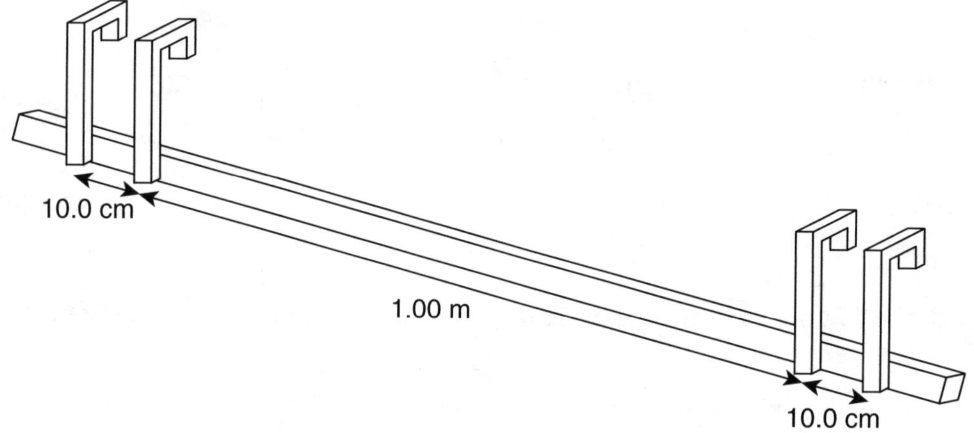

A metal cart slides along the track (with a constant acceleration), and each photogate records the time at which the cart passes through it as follows:

0 s	0.079 s	0.551 s	0.586 s

Which of the following best describes the acceleration of the cart?

Ⓐ 3.0 m/s^2

Ⓑ 7.0 m/s^2

Ⓒ 20 m/s^2

Ⓓ 35 m/s^2

43. Though oxygen most normally is found in diatomic form (O_2), it sometimes also occurs as monatomic oxygen (O) or as ozone (O_3). Which form would you expect to have the lowest specific heat (C_v)?

Ⓐ Monatomic oxygen

Ⓑ Diatomic oxygen

Ⓒ Ozone

Ⓓ All three forms should have the same specific heat.

44. Which of the following arrangements of four identical batteries should generate the highest voltage?

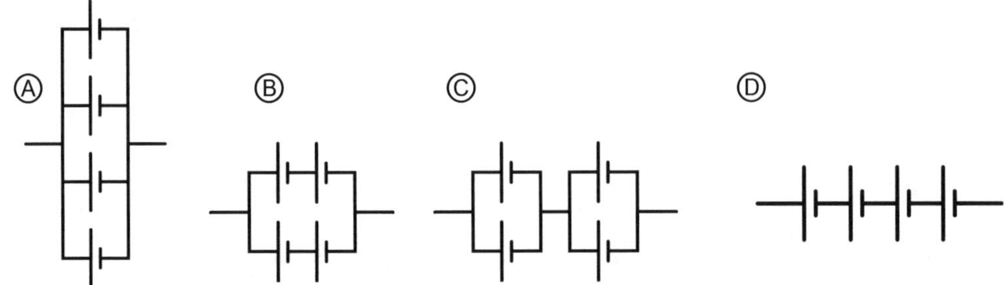

45. A train whistle has a frequency of 450 Hz (as heard by someone onboard the train). If the train is moving at 60 m/s, and the speed of sound is 340 m/s, what is the frequency in Hz, of the whistle as heard by someone standing in front of the train on a windless day? Record and bubble in your answer to the nearest tenth on the answer document.

46. The diagram to the right shows a simple DC electric motor, with the exception of the wires connecting it to the power source. To which part of the motor should those wires be attached?

Ⓐ To the north and south poles of the magnet

Ⓑ To the two sides of the commutator

Ⓒ To the ends of the coil

Ⓓ To the carbon brushes

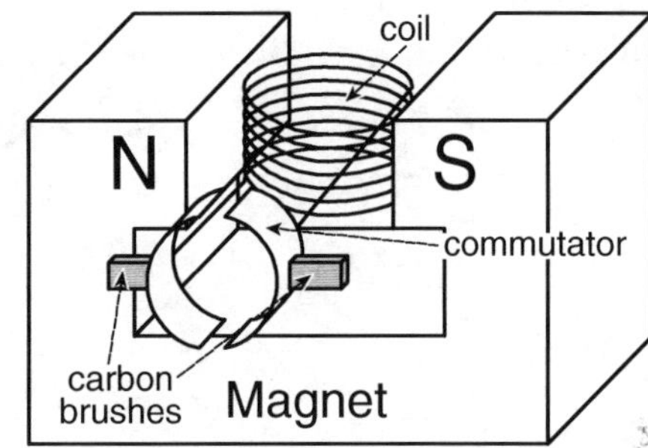

47. The photoelectric threshold frequency of gold is about 1.11×10^{15} Hz. A gold plate is configured so that a very sensitive ammeter measures the photoelectric current produced when light is shined on the plate. When an intense beam of light with a wavelength of 200 nm is directed at the gold plate, the ammeter measures a current of 2×10^{-6} A. What current would you expect to measure if a beam of light with half the intensity and twice the wavelength of the first beam is directed at the plate?

Ⓐ 4×10^{-6} A

Ⓑ 2×10^{-6} A

Ⓒ 1×10^{-6} A

Ⓓ 0 A

48. When a car brakes rapidly, passengers are thrown forward. Which physical law best describes why this occurs?

Ⓐ The law of conservation of energy

Ⓑ The law of entropy

Ⓒ The law of inertia

Ⓓ The law of relativity

49. A sled with a mass of 100 kg slides on an icy lake. It collides with another sled with a mass of 80 kg. Before the collision, the first sled was traveling at a speed of 4.0 m/s, and the second sled was stationary. After the collision, the first sled was traveling at a speed of 1.0 m/s. How fast was the second sled traveling after the collision?

Ⓐ 3.0 m/s

Ⓑ 3.8 m/s

Ⓒ 4.3 m/s

Ⓓ 5.0 m/s

50. Which of the following shows the correct way to connect an ammeter and a voltmeter to a circuit in order to measure the current through and voltage across a resistor?

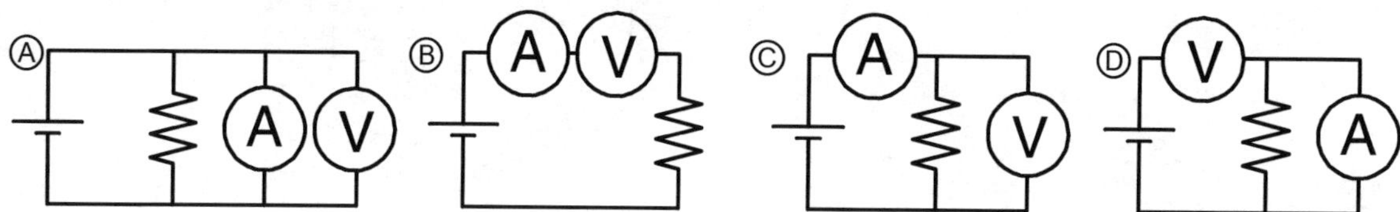

Answers and Explanations

1. C: The formula for velocity given constant acceleration is $v = v_0 + at$. Since the bicyclist starts from rest, $v_0 = 0$. So $v = (2\ m/s^2)\ (10\ s) = 20\ m/s$.

2. C: A wire needs to be made of a conductive material to allow electricity to flow through it easily. Wires are coated, however, in an insulating material so that the circuit will not be shorted if the wire comes into contact with itself or with another conductor.

3. B: During one full rotation, the horse travels a distance $2\pi r = 2(3.14)\ (1.5\ m) = 9.42\ m$. The speed is then equal to distance divided by time, 9.42 m/20 s = 0.47 m/s.

4. A: The temperature of a gas is related to the average kinetic energy of the component particles. If the molecule speed increases, the kinetic energy increases, and the temperature must also increase by definition. Any of the other choices *could* be true, depending on factors such as whether the gas is in a sealed and rigid container, but only choice A *must* be true.

5. 10.0: Consider the horizontal and vertical components of the motion separately. The initial velocity in the horizontal direction is (10 m/s) (cos 40°) = 7.66 m/s; the initial velocity in the vertical direction is (10 m/s) (sin 40°) = 6.43 m/s. We can use the vertical component to calculate the time the stone is in flight using the equation $x = x_0 + v_0t + ½at^2$, where x and x_0 are both 0 m (since the stone starts and ends at the same altitude), v_0 is 6.43 m/s, and a is the acceleration due to gravity, $-9.81\ m/s^2$. This yields $(6.43\ m/s)\ t = ½(9.81\ m/s^2)\ t2$; solving for t yields either $t = 0$ (corresponding to its initial position) or $t = 1.31$ s. Since there is no acceleration in the horizontal direction, the total horizontal distance the stone travels in this time is simply (7.66 m/s) (1.31 s) = 10.0 m.

6. D: The amplitude is in this case simply the maximum displacement from equilibrium (20 centimeters). The period is the time in which the point completes one full cycle (4 seconds), and the frequency is just the inverse of the period (0.25 Hz). To find the wavelength, however, information about a different point that corresponds to this one, or about the speed of the wave, is required and not given, and D is the correct choice.

7. A: In an action-reaction force pair, the reaction force must be exerted *by* the object *on* which the action force is exerted, and *on* the object *by* which the action force is exerted. Since the action force is exerted *by* the Earth *on* the rock, the reaction force must be exerted *by* the rock *on* the Earth. The only choice that fits this criterion is A: (Note that it would have been just as valid to consider the pull of the rock's gravity on the Earth to be the action force, and the pull of the Earth's gravity on the rock to be the reaction force. The important thing is there are two equal and opposite forces; which is the action and which is the reaction is essentially arbitrary.)

8. A: Coulomb developed the formula for electromagnetic force now known as Coulomb's Law. Faraday developed the idea of the electromagnetic field. Maxwell worked out the unification of electricity and magnetism as aspects of a single phenomenon. Bohr, however, is a more recent scientist best known for his work on the structure of atoms which helped lay the foundation for quantum mechanics, not for having played a major role in the study of electromagnetism, and the answer is A.

9. D: There are several different ways to approach this problem, but perhaps the simplest is by conservation of energy. On the flat stretch, we can take the car's gravitational potential energy as zero, so its mechanical energy is purely kinetic: $KE = \frac{1}{2}mv^2$. If the car just barely makes it to the top of the loop (like a projectile at the top of its arc), its velocity and therefore its kinetic energy are zero at that point, and its mechanical energy is purely gravitational potential energy: $PE = mgh$. Since energy is conserved, the energy at these two points must be equal: $\frac{1}{2}mv^2 = mgh$. The masses cancel, leaving $\frac{1}{2}v^2 = gh$, and solving for v yields $v = \sqrt{2gh} = \sqrt{2(9.8\text{m/s}^2)(10\text{m})} = \sqrt{196\text{m}^2/s^2} =$ 14 m/s.

10. B: The image of a distant object seen through a thin convex lens is real, because the light rays actually do converge at the location of the image, and inverted. The only choice with these characteristics is B: One way to see this is by tracing light rays, as in the following diagram (in which the black circles represent the focal length of the lens):

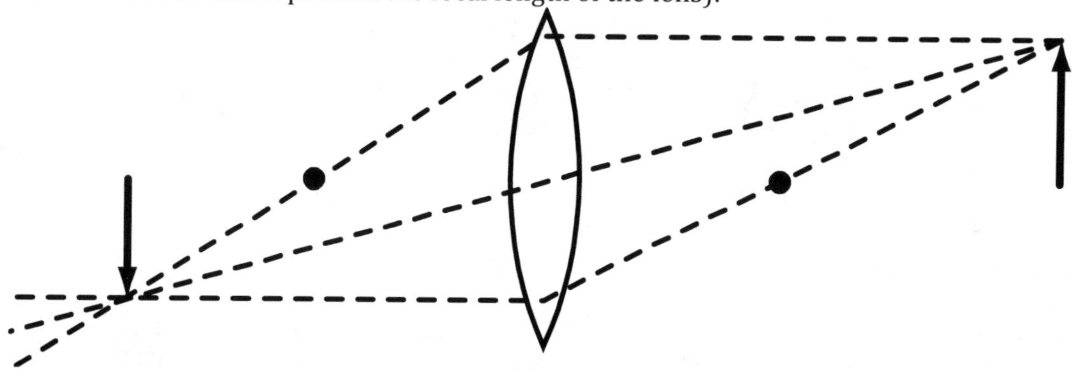

11. A: As described, there are two forces acting on the block: the tension in the spring pulling it upward, and the block's own weight (the force of gravity) pulling it downward. Only choice A depicts these forces correctly. Choice B has them acting in the wrong directions, choice C incorrectly adds velocity which is not a force and does not belong on a force diagram, and choice D combines the mistakes of B and C.

12. D: The equation for the gravitational force is $F = \frac{Gm_1m_2}{r^2}$. In order for the units to work out correctly and yield an answer in Newtons, r has to be in meters. We can easily convert, and 2.9×10^9 km = 2.9×10^{12} m. We then have $F = \frac{\left(6.67\times10^{-11}\frac{\text{m}^3}{\text{kg}\cdot\text{s}^2}\right)(8.7\times10^{25}\text{kg})(2.0\times10^{30}\text{kg})}{(2.9\times10^{12}\text{m})^2} = 1.38\times10^{21}$ N.

13. C: Net work done is determined by the change in energy. Since the crate is not moving in the initial or final state, the relevant energy is gravitational potential energy. From the ground, the final change in altitude of the crate is 6 meters, which corresponds to a potential energy change of $mg\Delta h$ = (1000 N)(6 m) = 6000 J, and the net work done by the crane is 6000 J, choice C: That the crane first raised the crate to an altitude of 10 m before lowering it to 6 m is irrelevant for finding the *net* work.

14. B: A transformer works by induced voltage; the varying voltage through the coil on one side induces a voltage in the coil in the other. The ratio of the voltages on the sides of an ideal transformer is equal to the ratio of the numbers of turns in the coils. In this case, there are 15 coils on the left-hand side, and 10 coils on the right-hand side, for a ratio of 15/10, or 1.5. This same ratio must hold between the voltages, so that $\frac{150\ V}{V_R} = 1.5$, giving a voltage on the right of $V_R = 100$ V.

15. 49 kWh: The total mass of the fully loaded elevator is equal to 500 kg + 1500 kg = 2000 kg. If the elevator is moving at 2.5 m/s, it moves 2.5 m in one second. The work done in that second is equal to the change in potential energy, which is $mg\Delta h$ = (2000 kg)(9.81 m/s^2)(2.5 m) = 49050 J. The power is equal to the work divided by the time, which is 49050 J/1 s = 49050 W, or 49 kW.

16. B: All the lines of the calcium spectrum are present in the unknown spectrum, including the notable low-wavelength lines not present in the mercury or sodium spectra. The double line at around 590 nm characteristic of the sodium spectrum is also present, so the sample must contain sodium. However, the lines from the mercury spectrum are *not* present in the unknown sample, most notably the easily recognizable triple line at about 580 nm. Therefore the unknown sample contains calcium and sodium, but does *not* contain mercury; this corresponds to choice B.

17. A: We would expect the velocity to increase over time at a constant rate. Although choice A shows what appears to be a decrease in velocity, it is actually increasing in the negative direction; as we expect, and the magnitude of the velocity is increasing, as the ball picks up speed rolling down the slope. Choice B shows the velocity starting with some non-zero magnitude which then decreases to zero, the opposite of our expectation, and is incorrect. Choice C shows the velocity slowing to zero and then increasing again, and choice D shows the velocity increasing from and then decreasing to zero. Neither of these two choices makes physical sense; they are also incorrect. Choice A is correct.

18. D: The impulse is equal to the change in momentum. The initial momentum is (0.4 kg)(1 m/s) = 0.4 kg·m/s towards the player. The final momentum is (0.4 kg)(8 m/s) = 3.2 kg·m/s in the opposite direction. The change is then 3.2 kg·m/s – (-0.4 kg·m/s), where the negative sign reflects the opposite directions), which equals 3.6 kg·m/s.

19. C: Light is an electromagnetic wave, and thus a transverse wave; its oscillation is perpendicular to its propagation. Sound is a longitudinal wave, alternating compressions and expansions of the medium it's traveling through. Choice C correctly represents this.

20. C: Since the ring isn't moving, the net force is zero. If we separate the force into perpendicular components, both components must be zero. If we consider the *x* direction to be to the right on the page, and the *y* direction to be upward, then one student is pulling completely in the +*x* direction, and another is pulling completely in the -*y* direction. Consider the *y* components first. One student is pulling with a force of 100 N in the -*y* direction, while another is pulling at an angle with a force of 115 N. The *y* components of these forces must cancel, and the *y* component of the 115 N force must be 100 N. This means the Pythagorean theorem can find the *x* component of the force at an angle: $\sqrt{(115\text{ N})^2 - (100\text{ N})^2}$ = 57 N in the -*x* direction. Since the *x* components of all the forces must also cancel, the unknown force must be 57 N in the +*x* direction, choice C.

21. B: Data is stored on cassette tapes by magnetizing the tapes. Compasses point north because of magnetic attraction to the Earth's magnetic pole. Maglev trains "float" because of magnetic repulsion between the trail and the rail. Choice B, compact discs, however, does not rely directly on magnetism, and is the correct choice; the data is stored in the form of small pits in the surface which affect the reflection of laser light.

22. A: Heat between objects in contact with each other is transferred by conduction, choice A: Convection is transfer by currents within a body of fluid, and radiation is the transfer of heat between objects *not* in contact, through light rays emitted by the hotter object and absorbed by the cooler one.

23. D: Sound cannot travel through a vacuum, though it doesn't necessarily follow that it *can* travel through solids. Nor does the fact sound can travel through a solid follow from the fact that the atoms are packed tightly together. The fact that a sound is produced by knocking on a solid object also does not prove sound can pass through the object. However, if you hear a sound on the other side of a solid wall, the sound must have traveled through the wall. Choice D is the best answer.

24. A: The cannonball's horizontal distance is not specified, but the horizontal and vertical components can be independently considered; this problem can be approached by considering only the vertical motion, and the easiest approach depends on recognizing the cannonball will reach its peak altitude exactly halfway through its arc. Thus, if the full trajectory takes four seconds, the cannonball takes two seconds to reach its peak, and two seconds to fall back to the ground. Knowing this, a formula for uniformly accelerated motion will calculate how high the cannonball could fall from in two seconds: $x - x_0 = v_0t + ½at^2 = ½(9.8 \text{ m/s}^2)(2 \text{ s})^2 = 19.6 \text{ m}$, (recognizing that v_0 is zero at the top of the arc).

25. 633 nm: The speed of a wave is equal to wavelength times frequency, $v = f\lambda$. The speed of a light wave is $c = 3.00\times10^8$ m/s. The wavelength is therefore equal to $c / f =$ $(3.00\times10^8 \text{ m/s}) / (4.74\times10^{14} \text{ Hz}) = 6.33\times10^{-7}$ m, or 633 nm.

26. B: The effective resistance of two or more resistors in parallel is equal to the reciprocal of the sum of their reciprocal resistances. The two resistors in parallel therefore have an effective resistance of $((200\Omega)^{-1} + (500\ \Omega)^{-1})^{-1} = 142.9\ \Omega$. Resistances in series simply sum, so the total resistance of the parallel element plus the second 200 Ω resistor is 142.9 Ω + 200 Ω = 342.9 Ω. Ohm's Law, $V = IR$, can be used to solve for $I = (12 \text{ V})/(342.9\ \Omega) = 0.035 \text{ A} = 35 \text{ mA}$.

27. D: Conservation laws of mass and momentum do not apply here. The law of entropy is also known as the second law of thermodynamics, and can be stated in several different forms. One form, first developed by Lord Kelvin, states that it is impossible to convert heat into useful energy without producing more heat energy at another point in the system to heat up a low-temperature sink. If the air is cooled to a lower temperature than the plane, the heat energy is being converted into work without such a side effect, and although conservation of energy is not violated, the law of entropy is, and choice D is correct.

28. C: If the 200 kg barrel has an acceleration of 0.13 m/s², the net force on the barrel is $\sum F = ma =$ $(200 \text{ kg})(0.13 \text{ m/s}^2) = 26$ N. Since Jim is exerting a force of 320 N, there must be a force working against him with a magnitude of 320 N – 26 N = 294 N.

29. D: The force binding quarks into protons, and nucleons into nuclei, is the strong nuclear force. Electrons are attracted to protons by the electromagnetic force. However, it is the weak nuclear force, choice D that governs the decay of subatomic particles, for example the decay of a neutron into a proton, an electron, and a neutrino.

30. A: The energy released by the reaction cannot have been created out of nothing, but has to have come from somewhere or something. In this case, some of the mass of the particles is converted into energy, according to the mass-energy equivalence relation, $E=mc^2$. Since some mass is therefore lost, the total mass before the reaction (the total mass of the hydrogen nuclei) must be slightly larger than the total mass after the reaction (the mass of the helium nucleus); this is expressed in choice A:

31. C: To find the magnitude of the electromagnetic force use Coulomb's Law, $F = \frac{kq_1q_2}{r^2}$. Clearly, the masses do not actually enter into this equation, and they are not needed here. The charge of a proton is equal in magnitude of the electron's but of opposite polarity. So we have $F = \frac{(8.99\times10^9 \text{ N}\cdot\text{m}^2/\text{C}^2)(-1.6\times10^{-19}\text{ C})(1.6\times10^{-19}\text{ C})}{(1\times10^{-4}\text{ m})^2} = -2.3\times10^{-20}$ N. (Since we are asked for the magnitude of the force, we can ignore the negative sign.)

32. C: To find the speed of the torpedo relative to the island, the speed of the submarine relative to the island must be added to the speed of the torpedo relative to the submarine. However, since these velocities are not in the same direction, they must be added as *vectors*:

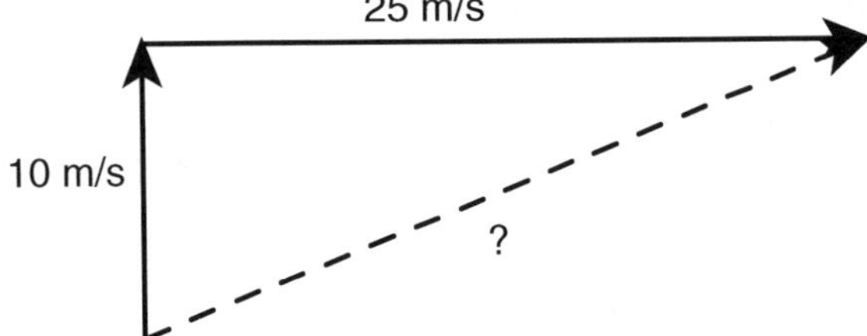

The missing velocity can be found by using the Pythagorean theorem: $x = \sqrt{(10\text{ m/s})^2 + (25\text{ m/s})^2}$ ≈ 27 m/s.

33. B: Refraction is governed by Snell's law, $n_1 \sin\theta_1 = n_2 \sin\theta_2$. If n_1 is defined to be the index of refraction of air, and n_2 the index of refraction of amber, Snell's law yields $n_1 \sin 32° = n_2 \sin 20°$. Solving for n_2 using the fact the index of refraction of air is very close to 1 yields $n_2 = \sin 32° / \sin 20° = 1.55$. Note these calculations must be performed in degree mode rather than radian.

34. D: The problem does not specify in what reference frame the speed of the suitcase should be measured. As such, the problem does not have a unique answer. Relative to the man the speed of the suitcase is 0 m/s; to the bus it is 1 m/s; to the street, it is 9 m/s. Since not enough information is provided, D is the best choice.

35. 163.3 m/s: If the rockets are identical and have the same efficiency, the same amount of energy goes into propelling each rocket. The changes in their mechanical energies should be equal. Since their gravitational potential energies do not change, their final kinetic energies must be equal. The first rocket has a kinetic energy of $\frac{1}{2}mv^2 = \frac{1}{2}(1000\text{ kg})(200\text{ m/s})^2 = 2.00\times10^7$ J. Equating this energy to that of the second rocket yields $\frac{1}{2}(1500\text{ kg})v_2^2 = 2.00\times10^7$ J. Solving for v_2 yields a speed of 163.3 m/s.

36. A: X-rays have a short wavelength (several orders of magnitude shorter than the wavelength of visible light), which rules out choices B and D: Choice C is true – photons with a shorter wavelength *do* have higher energies – but does not explain why x-rays are used in medical imaging. (If anything, the higher energy would seem to be a *dis*advantage for medical imaging, since it would mean a greater chance of tissue damage.) Only choice A accurately explains why x-rays are used in medical imaging.

37. D: When two quantities are multiplied or divided, the squares of their relative errors add. That is, if $Z = XY$, $\left(\frac{\Delta Z}{Z}\right)^2 = \left(\frac{\Delta X}{X}\right)^2 + \left(\frac{\Delta Y}{Y}\right)^2$. Absolute error for a measuring device is considered to be one half of the smallest unit that it can measure. In this case, since the meter stick measures to the nearest millimeter, it may be off by as much as half a millimeter. Since the stopwatch measures to the nearest 0.01 seconds, it may be off by as much as 0.005 seconds. Plugging these values into the equation yields $\left(\frac{\Delta v}{v}\right)^2 = \left(\frac{0.0005\text{ m}}{1\text{ m}}\right)^2 + \left(\frac{0.005\text{ s}}{5\text{ s}}\right)^2 = 1.25 \times 10^{-6}$. To solve for Δv, take the square root of both sides and multiply by v: $\Delta v = 0.000224$. This narrows the choice to A and D. When two quantities are multiplied or divided, the number of significant figures in the result is equal to the least number of significant figures in each quantity. In this case, the time measurement has three; therefore, answer D is the correct choice.

38. C: In 1968, Sheldon Glashow, Abdus Salam, and Steven Weinberg developed a theory that united electricity and the weak nuclear force as manifestations of a unified electroweak interaction. The strong nuclear force was later coordinated with the electroweak interaction in the standard model of particle physics. Physicists have yet to discover a fully satisfactory theory that combines the gravitational force with the other three. Choice C is correct.

39. D: The work done on an object is equal to its total change in energy, including the change in potential energy. If an object's potential energy increases, then the work done is greater than the change in the kinetic energy (since ΔKE + ΔPE > ΔKE). If the object's potential energy decreases, then the work done is less than the change in the kinetic energy (since ΔKE + ΔPE < ΔKE). If only the kinetic energy changes, then the work done is equal to the change in kinetic energy. Since no further information is given, D is the correct choice.

40. B: While objects could be targeted by singular photons, this does not relate to the microscope's function. The uncertainty principle, if anything, would prevent knowledge of exact contours, and quantum entanglement refers to objects expressible by the same wavefunction and is not applicable to the observer. Electron microscopes instead work because the electron beam "illuminates" the observed object in a manner analogous to the way visible light illuminates objects in an optical microscope; that is, by reflecting from and being diffracted by the objects, and B is correct. The reason that electron microscopes can yield much higher magnifications is because electrons have a much smaller wavelength than visible light.

41. B: Choice D would violate the law of conservation of energy. If the chemicals heat up, their temperatures increase, and their kinetic energies therefore increase, so energy could not have been obtained from kinetic energy, so choice A is incorrect. Nor do chemical reactions typically involve absorption of heat from the environment as stated by choice C: Choice B correctly describes the situation: chemical bonds contain some amount of potential energy, which may be released in certain chemical reactions.

42. A: Acceleration is equal to change in velocity, and can be obtained by determining the velocity of the cart at two points along the track. The best choice is to find the velocity between the first two photogates and between the last two photogates. For each of these, we can use $v = \Delta x/\Delta t$: between the first two photogates, v_1 = 0.100 m / (0.079 s – 0 s) = 1.27 m/s, and between the second two, v_2 = 0.100 m / (0.586 s – 0.551 s) = 2.86 m/s. From here, there are at least two approaches to get an approximate answer for the acceleration, either the formula $v_2^2 = v_1^2+2ax$, solved for a to get a = ((2.86 m/s)^2 – (1.27 m/s)^2)/2(1.00 m) = 3.3 m/s^2, or the formula $v_2 = v_1 + at$, setting t equal to the time it takes to pass from the second to the third photogate (0.551 s – 0.079 s = 0.472 s) and solving for a to get a = (2.86 m/s – 1.27 m/s)/(0.472 s) = 3.4 m/s^2. While these answers don't exactly match any of the given choices, they are clearly closest to choice A.

Although this approximate result is good enough to select the correct choice, we can get a more accurate answer by taking into account that the velocities we calculated aren't really the velocities at the point the cart passes the second and third photogates; they are respectively the average

velocity between the first and second photogates, and the average velocity between the third and fourth. These average velocities, however, are equal to the instantaneous velocities at the halfway point (with respect to time, not distance) of each interval. The halfway point of the first interval is the time
t_1 = (0 s + 0.079 s)/2 = 0.0395 s, and for the second interval, t_2 = (0.551 s + 0.586 s)/2 = 0.5685 s. We can then use t = 0.569 s – 0.040 s = 0.0529 s, and a = (0.286 m/s – 0.127 m/s)/(0.529 s) = 3.0 m/s^2.

43. A: The specific heat of a substance depends mainly on the number of degrees of freedom of its molecules. All else being equal, a diatomic molecule tends to have more degrees of freedom, and hence a higher specific heat, than a monatomic molecule. A molecule with three atoms, such as ozone, should tend to have still more degrees of freedom, and a still higher specific heat. Therefore, we would expect monatomic oxygen to have a lower specific heat than either diatomic oxygen or ozone; this is expressed by choice A.

44. D: Voltages are equal in parallel and sum in series. An arrangement of identical batteries placed in parallel yields only the voltage of one battery. (This arrangement would, however, have a larger capacity, and hence would last longer than a single battery.) An array of identical batteries placed in series yield the total voltage of all the batteries. Arrangement A shows four batteries in parallel, yields the voltage of a single battery. Arrangement B shows two batteries in series, in parallel with another two batteries in series, and arrangement C shows the opposite, with two batteries in parallel, in series with another two in parallel. Each pair of batteries in series yields the voltage of two batteries, but only the voltage of one pair when put in parallel. Each pair of batteries in parallel yields the voltage of a single battery; two such pairs put in series yields the voltage of two batteries. All the batteries in arrangement D are in series, so arrangement D yields the voltage of four batteries, the highest of the four choices.

45. 546.4 Hz: The general equation for the Doppler frequency is $f = \frac{(v+v_r)}{(v+v_s)} f_0$, where v is the velocity of the wave through the medium (in this case, the speed of sound), and v_r and v_s are respectively the speed of the receiver and of the source relative to the medium. In this case, the receiver (the person standing in front of the train) is stationary relative to the medium (the air), so $v_r = 0$. Since the source is moving toward the receiver, v_s is negative. That yields
$f = \frac{(340\text{ m/s})}{(340\text{ m/s}-60\text{ m/s})}$ 450 Hz = 546.4 Hz.

46. D: An electric motor works because the magnetic field generated by the magnet produces a force on the current-carrying coil, causing it to rotate. However, when the coil is aligned parallel to the field, the force will vanish, and the rotation will stop. Even if the coil's rotational momentum makes it overshoot this position a little, the magnetic force will tend to rotate it back the other way. To prevent this and make the coil continue rotating, the ends of the coil are attached to a commutator that comes into contact with the power source through stationary brushes. When the coil's rotation passes the halfway point, the brushes will pass the gap in the commutator, and each brush will now be in contact with the opposite end of the coil, causing the current in the coil to reverse direction, which means the magnetic force will again be in such a direction as to continue causing rotation in the same direction. For this to work, it is essential that the power source be connected to the brushes, not to the commutator or to the coil directly. (Connecting the power source to the magnet would not do anything.) D is correct.

47. D: Twice the initial wavelength would be 400 nm. This light would have a frequency of $f = c / \lambda$

= $(3\times10^8$ m/s) / $(4\times10^{-7}$ m) = 7.5×10^{14} Hz. This is below the threshold frequency of 1.11×10^{15} Hz, so regardless of the light's intensity no electrons will be ejected, and no current will be produced.

48. C: The passengers are thrown forward because of their inertia; in the absence of an external force, they tend to preserve their state of motion (in this case, in the direction of the car's movement), even if the car around them stops. (Of course, they will eventually encounter external forces that will stop them, such as the tension in their seatbelts.) Although this manifests as a short continuation of existing kinetic energy, the energy conservation law is not governing the phenomenon, nor certainly are entropic or relativistic laws. Choice C is correct.

49. B: Since no information is given about how elastic the collision was, it is safest to avoid appealing to conservation of kinetic energy, but this problem can be solved using conservation of momentum. Before the collision, the total momentum is (100 kg)(4.0 m/s) = 400 kg·m/s. (The second sled's initial velocity is zero, so it has no momentum.) After the collision, the first sled's momentum is (100 kg)(1.0 m/s) = 100 kg·m/s. Since the total momentum is conserved, the second sled's momentum must then be 400 kg·m/s – 100 kg·m/s = 300 kg·m/s, and its speed must be (300 kg·m/s) / (80 kg) = 3.8 m/s.

50. C: An ammeter has a very low resistance, the better to cause current to flow through it freely. Placing an ammeter in parallel with another circuit element (as in choices A and D) will cause almost all the current to go through the ammeter instead of the circuit element, essentially creating a short circuit, leading to, at best inaccurate readings. It should therefore always be placed in series with the element through which the current is being measured. A voltmeter, on the other hand, has a very high resistance and should always be placed in parallel with the element across which the voltage is being measured. Placing a voltmeter in series with another circuit element (as in choices B and D) will lead to an essentially open circuit and, again, at best give inaccurate readings. The only diagram that correctly shows the ammeter in series and the voltmeter in parallel is choice C.

Secret Key #1 - Time is Your Greatest Enemy

Pace Yourself

Wear a watch. At the beginning of the test, check the time (or start a chronometer on your watch to count the minutes), and check the time after every few questions to make sure you are "on schedule."

If you are forced to speed up, do it efficiently. Usually one or more answer choices can be eliminated without too much difficulty. Above all, don't panic. Don't speed up and just begin guessing at random choices. By pacing yourself, and continually monitoring your progress against your watch, you will always know exactly how far ahead or behind you are with your available time. If you find that you are one minute behind on the test, don't skip one question without spending any time on it, just to catch back up. Take 15 fewer seconds on the next four questions, and after four questions you'll have caught back up. Once you catch back up, you can continue working each problem at your normal pace.

Furthermore, don't dwell on the problems that you were rushed on. If a problem was taking up too much time and you made a hurried guess, it must be difficult. The difficult questions are the ones you are most likely to miss anyway, so it isn't a big loss. It is better to end with more time than you need than to run out of time.

Lastly, sometimes it is beneficial to slow down if you are constantly getting ahead of time. You are always more likely to catch a careless mistake by working more slowly than quickly, and among very high-scoring test takers (those who are likely to have lots of time left over), careless errors affect the score more than mastery of material.

Secret Key #2 - Guessing is not Guesswork

You probably know that guessing is a good idea. Unlike other standardized tests, there is no penalty for getting a wrong answer. Even if you have no idea about a question, you still have a 20-25% chance of getting it right.

Most test takers do not understand the impact that proper guessing can have on their score. Unless you score extremely high, guessing will significantly contribute to your final score.

Monkeys Take the Test

What most test takers don't realize is that to insure that 20-25% chance, you have to guess randomly. If you put 20 monkeys in a room to take this test, assuming they answered once per question and behaved themselves, on average they would get 20-25% of the questions correct. Put 20 test takers in the room, and the average will be much lower among guessed questions. Why?

1. The test writers intentionally write deceptive answer choices that "look" right. A test taker has no idea about a question, so he picks the "best looking" answer, which is often wrong. The monkey has no idea what looks good and what doesn't, so it will consistently be right

about 20-25% of the time.

2. Test takers will eliminate answer choices from the guessing pool based on a hunch or intuition. Simple but correct answers often get excluded, leaving a 0% chance of being correct. The monkey has no clue, and often gets lucky with the best choice.

This is why the process of elimination endorsed by most test courses is flawed and detrimental to your performance. Test takers don't guess; they make an ignorant stab in the dark that is usually worse than random.

$5 Challenge

Let me introduce one of the most valuable ideas of this course—the $5 challenge:

- *You only mark your "best guess" if you are willing to bet $5 on it.*
- *You only eliminate choices from guessing if you are willing to bet $5 on it.*

Why $5? Five dollars is an amount of money that is small yet not insignificant, and can really add up fast (20 questions could cost you $100). Likewise, each answer choice on one question of the test will have a small impact on your overall score, but it can really add up to a lot of points in the end.

The process of elimination IS valuable. The following shows your chance of guessing it right:

If you eliminate wrong answer choices until only this many remain:	Chance of getting it correct:
1	100%
2	50%
3	33%

However, if you accidentally eliminate the right answer or go on a hunch for an incorrect answer, your chances drop dramatically—to 0%. By guessing among all the answer choices, you are GUARANTEED to have a shot at the right answer.

That's why the $5 test is so valuable. If you give up the advantage and safety of a pure guess, it had better be worth the risk.

What we still haven't covered is how to be sure that whatever guess you make is truly random. Here's the easiest way:

- *Always pick the first answer choice among those remaining.*

Such a technique means that you have decided, **before you see a single test question**, exactly how you are going to guess, and since the order of choices tells you nothing about which one is correct, this guessing technique is perfectly random.

This section is not meant to scare you away from making educated guesses or eliminating choices; you just need to define when a choice is worth eliminating. The $5 test, along with a pre-defined random guessing strategy, is the best way to make sure you reap all of the benefits of guessing.

Secret Key #3 - Practice Smarter, Not Harder

Many test takers delay the test preparation process because they dread the awful amounts of practice time they think necessary to succeed on the test. We have refined an effective method that will take you only a fraction of the time.

There are a number of "obstacles" in the path to success. Among these are answering questions, finishing in time, and mastering test-taking strategies. All must be executed on the day of the test at peak performance, or your score will suffer. The test is a mental marathon that has a large impact on your future.

Just like a marathon runner, it is important to work your way up to the full challenge. So first you just worry about questions, and then time, and finally strategy:

Success Strategy

1. Find a good source for practice tests.
2. If you are willing to make a larger time investment, consider using more than one study guide. Often the different approaches of multiple authors will help you "get" difficult concepts.
3. Take a practice test with no time constraints, with all study helps, "open book." Take your time with questions and focus on applying strategies.
4. Take a practice test with time constraints, with all guides, "open book."
5. Take a final practice test without open material and with time limits.

If you have time to take more practice tests, just repeat step 5. By gradually exposing yourself to the full rigors of the test environment, you will condition your mind to the stress of test day and maximize your success.

Secret Key #4 - Prepare, Don't Procrastinate

Let me state an obvious fact: if you take the test three times, you will probably get three different scores. This is due to the way you feel on test day, the level of preparedness you have, and the version of the test you see. Despite the test writers' claims to the contrary, some versions of the test WILL be easier for you than others.

Since your future depends so much on your score, you should maximize your chances of success. In order to maximize the likelihood of success, you've got to prepare in advance. This means taking practice tests and spending time learning the information and test taking strategies you will need to succeed.

Never go take the actual test as a "practice" test, expecting that you can just take it again if you need to. Take all the practice tests you can on your own, but when you go to take the official test, be prepared, be focused, and do your best the first time!

Secret Key #5 - Test Yourself

Everyone knows that time is money. There is no need to spend too much of your time or too little of your time preparing for the test. You should only spend as much of your precious time preparing as is necessary for you to get the score you need.

Once you have taken a practice test under real conditions of time constraints, then you will know if you are ready for the test or not.

If you have scored extremely high the first time that you take the practice test, then there is not much point in spending countless hours studying. You are already there.

Benchmark your abilities by retaking practice tests and seeing how much you have improved. Once you consistently score high enough to guarantee success, then you are ready.

If you have scored well below where you need, then knuckle down and begin studying in earnest. Check your improvement regularly through the use of practice tests under real conditions. Above all, don't worry, panic, or give up. The key is perseverance!

Then, when you go to take the test, remain confident and remember how well you did on the practice tests. If you can score high enough on a practice test, then you can do the same on the real thing.

General Strategies

The most important thing you can do is to ignore your fears and jump into the test immediately. Do not be overwhelmed by any strange-sounding terms. You have to jump into the test like jumping into a pool—all at once is the easiest way.

Make Predictions

As you read and understand the question, try to guess what the answer will be. Remember that several of the answer choices are wrong, and once you begin reading them, your mind will immediately become cluttered with answer choices designed to throw you off. Your mind is typically the most focused immediately after you have read the question and digested its contents. If you can, try to predict what the correct answer will be. You may be surprised at what you can predict.

Quickly scan the choices and see if your prediction is in the listed answer choices. If it is, then you can be quite confident that you have the right answer. It still won't hurt to check the other answer choices, but most of the time, you've got it!

Answer the Question

It may seem obvious to only pick answer choices that answer the question, but the test writers can create some excellent answer choices that are wrong. Don't pick an answer just because it sounds right, or you believe it to be true. It MUST answer the question. Once you've made your selection, always go back and check it against the question and make sure that you didn't misread the question and that the answer choice does answer the question posed.

Benchmark

After you read the first answer choice, decide if you think it sounds correct or not. If it doesn't, move on to the next answer choice. If it does, mentally mark that answer choice. This doesn't mean that you've definitely selected it as your answer choice, it just means that it's the best you've seen thus far. Go ahead and read the next choice. If the next choice is worse than the one you've already selected, keep going to the next answer choice. If the next choice is better than the choice you've already selected, mentally mark the new answer choice as your best guess.

The first answer choice that you select becomes your standard. Every other answer choice must be benchmarked against that standard. That choice is correct until proven otherwise by another answer choice beating it out. Once you've decided that no other answer choice seems as good, do one final check to ensure that your answer choice answers the question posed.

Valid Information

Don't discount any of the information provided in the question. Every piece of information may be necessary to determine the correct answer. None of the information in the question is there to throw you off (while the answer choices will certainly have information to throw you off). If two seemingly unrelated topics are discussed, don't ignore either. You can be confident there is a relationship, or it wouldn't be included in the question, and you are probably going to have to determine what is that relationship to find the answer.

Avoid "Fact Traps"

Don't get distracted by a choice that is factually true. Your search is for the answer that answers the question. Stay focused and don't fall for an answer that is true but irrelevant. Always go back to the question and make sure you're choosing an answer that actually answers the question and is not just a true statement. An answer can be factually correct, but it MUST answer the question asked. Additionally, two answers can both be seemingly correct, so be sure to read all of the answer choices, and make sure that you get the one that BEST answers the question.

Milk the Question

Some of the questions may throw you completely off. They might deal with a subject you have not been exposed to, or one that you haven't reviewed in years. While your lack of knowledge about the subject will be a hindrance, the question itself can give you many clues that will help you find the correct answer. Read the question carefully and look for clues. Watch particularly for adjectives and nouns describing difficult terms or words that you don't recognize. Regardless of whether you completely understand a word or not, replacing it with a synonym, either provided or one you more familiar with, may help you to understand what the questions are asking. Rather than wracking your mind about specific detailed information concerning a difficult term or word, try to use mental substitutes that are easier to understand.

The Trap of Familiarity

Don't just choose a word because you recognize it. On difficult questions, you may not recognize a number of words in the answer choices. The test writers don't put "make-believe" words on the test, so don't think that just because you only recognize all the words in one answer choice that that answer choice must be correct. If you only recognize words in one answer choice, then focus on that one. Is it correct? Try your best to determine if it is correct. If it is, that's great. If not, eliminate it. Each word and answer choice you eliminate increases your chances of getting the question correct, even if you then have to guess among the unfamiliar choices.

Eliminate Answers

Eliminate choices as soon as you realize they are wrong. But be careful! Make sure you consider all of the possible answer choices. Just because one appears right, doesn't mean that the next one won't be even better! The test writers will usually put more than one good answer choice for every question, so read all of them. Don't worry if you are stuck between two that seem right. By getting down to just two remaining possible choices, your odds are now 50/50. Rather than wasting too much time, play the odds. You are guessing, but guessing wisely because you've been able to knock out some of the answer choices that you know are wrong. If you are eliminating choices and realize that the last answer choice you are left with is also obviously wrong, don't panic. Start over and consider each choice again. There may easily be something that you missed the first time and will realize on the second pass.

Tough Questions

If you are stumped on a problem or it appears too hard or too difficult, don't waste time. Move on! Remember though, if you can quickly check for obviously incorrect answer choices, your chances of guessing correctly are greatly improved. Before you completely give up, at least try to knock out a couple of possible answers. Eliminate what you can and then guess at the remaining answer choices before moving on.

Brainstorm

If you get stuck on a difficult question, spend a few seconds quickly brainstorming. Run through the complete list of possible answer choices. Look at each choice and ask yourself, "Could this answer the question satisfactorily?" Go through each answer choice and consider it independently of the others. By systematically going through all possibilities, you may find something that you would otherwise overlook. Remember though that when you get stuck, it's important to try to keep moving.

Read Carefully

Understand the problem. Read the question and answer choices carefully. Don't miss the question because you misread the terms. You have plenty of time to read each question thoroughly and make sure you understand what is being asked. Yet a happy medium must be attained, so don't waste too much time. You must read carefully, but efficiently.

Face Value

When in doubt, use common sense. Always accept the situation in the problem at face value. Don't read too much into it. These problems will not require you to make huge leaps of logic. The test writers aren't trying to throw you off with a cheap trick. If you have to go beyond creativity and make a leap of logic in order to have an answer choice answer the question, then you should look at the other answer choices. Don't overcomplicate the problem by creating theoretical relationships or explanations that will warp time or space. These are normal problems rooted in reality. It's just that the applicable relationship or explanation may not be readily apparent and you have to figure things out. Use your common sense to interpret anything that isn't clear.

Prefixes

If you're having trouble with a word in the question or answer choices, try dissecting it. Take advantage of every clue that the word might include. Prefixes and suffixes can be a huge help. Usually they allow you to determine a basic meaning. Pre- means before, post- means after, pro - is positive, de- is negative. From these prefixes and suffixes, you can get an idea of the general meaning of the word and try to put it into context. Beware though of any traps. Just because con- is the opposite of pro-, doesn't necessarily mean congress is the opposite of progress!

Hedge Phrases

Watch out for critical hedge phrases, led off with words such as "likely," "may," "can," "sometimes," "often," "almost," "mostly," "usually," "generally," "rarely," and "sometimes." Question writers insert these hedge phrases to cover every possibility. Often an answer choice will be wrong simply because it leaves no room for exception. Unless the situation calls for them, avoid answer choices that have definitive words like "exactly," and "always."

Switchback Words

Stay alert for "switchbacks." These are the words and phrases frequently used to alert you to shifts in thought. The most common switchback word is "but." Others include "although," "however," "nevertheless," "on the other hand," "even though," "while," "in spite of," "despite," and "regardless of."

New Information

Correct answer choices will rarely have completely new information included. Answer choices typically are straightforward reflections of the material asked about and will directly relate to the question. If a new piece of information is included in an answer choice that doesn't even seem to relate to the topic being asked about, then that answer choice is likely incorrect. All of the information needed to answer the question is usually provided for you in the question. You should not have to make guesses that are unsupported or choose answer choices that require unknown information that cannot be reasoned from what is given.

Time Management

On technical questions, don't get lost on the technical terms. Don't spend too much time on any one question. If you don't know what a term means, then odds are you aren't going to get much further since you don't have a dictionary. You should be able to immediately recognize whether or not you know a term. If you don't, work with the other clues that you have—the other answer choices and terms provided—but don't waste too much time trying to figure out a difficult term that you don't know.

Contextual Clues

Look for contextual clues. An answer can be right but not the correct answer. The contextual clues will help you find the answer that is most right and is correct. Understand the context in which a phrase or statement is made. This will help you make important distinctions.

Don't Panic

Panicking will not answer any questions for you; therefore, it isn't helpful. When you first see the question, if your mind goes blank, take a deep breath. Force yourself to mechanically go through the steps of solving the problem using the strategies you've learned.

Pace Yourself

Don't get clock fever. It's easy to be overwhelmed when you're looking at a page full of questions, your mind is full of random thoughts and feeling confused, and the clock is ticking down faster than you would like. Calm down and maintain the pace that you have set for yourself. As long as you are on track by monitoring your pace, you are guaranteed to have enough time for yourself. When you get to the last few minutes of the test, it may seem like you won't have enough time left, but if you only have as many questions as you should have left at that point, then you're right on track!

Answer Selection

The best way to pick an answer choice is to eliminate all of those that are wrong, until only one is left and confirm that is the correct answer. Sometimes though, an answer choice may immediately look right. Be careful! Take a second to make sure that the other choices are not equally obvious. Don't make a hasty mistake. There are only two times that you should stop before checking other answers. First is when you are positive that the answer choice you have selected is correct. Second is when time is almost out and you have to make a quick guess!

Check Your Work

Since you will probably not know every term listed and the answer to every question, it is important that you get credit for the ones that you do know. Don't miss any questions through careless mistakes. If at all possible, try to take a second to look back over your answer selection and make sure you've selected the correct answer choice and haven't made a costly careless mistake (such as marking an answer choice that you didn't mean to mark). The time it takes for this quick double check should more than pay for itself in caught mistakes.

Beware of Directly Quoted Answers

Sometimes an answer choice will repeat word for word a portion of the question or reference section. However, beware of such exact duplication. It may be a trap! More than likely, the correct choice will paraphrase or summarize a point, rather than being exactly the same wording.

Slang

Scientific sounding answers are better than slang ones. An answer choice that begins "To compare the outcomes..." is much more likely to be correct than one that begins "Because some people insisted..."

Extreme Statements

Avoid wild answers that throw out highly controversial ideas that are proclaimed as established fact. An answer choice that states the "process should used in certain situations, if..." is much more likely to be correct than one that states the "process should be discontinued completely." The first is a calm rational statement and doesn't even make a definitive, uncompromising stance, using a hedge word "if" to provide wiggle room, whereas the second choice is a radical idea and far more extreme.

Answer Choice Families

When you have two or more answer choices that are direct opposites or parallels, one of them is usually the correct answer. For instance, if one answer choice states "x increases" and another answer choice states "x decreases" or "y increases," then those two or three answer choices are very similar in construction and fall into the same family of answer choices. A family of answer choices consists of two or three answer choices, very similar in construction, but often with directly opposite meanings. Usually the correct answer choice will be in that family of answer choices. The "odd man out" or answer choice that doesn't seem to fit the parallel construction of the other answer choices is more likely to be incorrect.

Special Report: How to Overcome Test Anxiety

The very nature of tests caters to some level of anxiety, nervousness, or tension, just as we feel for any important event that occurs in our lives. A little bit of anxiety or nervousness can be a good thing. It helps us with motivation, and makes achievement just that much sweeter. However, too much anxiety can be a problem, especially if it hinders our ability to function and perform.

"Test anxiety," is the term that refers to the emotional reactions that some test-takers experience when faced with a test or exam. Having a fear of testing and exams is based upon a rational fear, since the test-taker's performance can shape the course of an academic career. Nevertheless, experiencing excessive fear of examinations will only interfere with the test-taker's ability to perform and chance to be successful.

There are a large variety of causes that can contribute to the development and sensation of test anxiety. These include, but are not limited to, lack of preparation and worrying about issues surrounding the test.

Lack of Preparation

Lack of preparation can be identified by the following behaviors or situations:

- Not scheduling enough time to study, and therefore cramming the night before the test or exam
- Managing time poorly, to create the sensation that there is not enough time to do everything
- Failing to organize the text information in advance, so that the study material consists of the entire text and not simply the pertinent information
- Poor overall studying habits

Worrying, on the other hand, can be related to both the test taker, or many other factors around him/her that will be affected by the results of the test. These include worrying about:

- Previous performances on similar exams, or exams in general
- How friends and other students are achieving
- The negative consequences that will result from a poor grade or failure

There are three primary elements to test anxiety. Physical components, which involve the same typical bodily reactions as those to acute anxiety (to be discussed below). Emotional factors have to do with fear or panic. Mental or cognitive issues concerning attention spans and memory abilities.

Physical Signals

There are many different symptoms of test anxiety, and these are not limited to mental and emotional strain. Frequently there are a range of physical signals that will let a test taker know that he/she is suffering from test anxiety. These bodily changes can include the following:

- Perspiring
- Sweaty palms
- Wet, trembling hands
- Nausea
- Dry mouth
- A knot in the stomach
- Headache
- Faintness
- Muscle tension
- Aching shoulders, back and neck
- Rapid heart beat
- Feeling too hot/cold

To recognize the sensation of test anxiety, a test-taker should monitor him/herself for the following sensations:

- The physical distress symptoms as listed above
- Emotional sensitivity, expressing emotional feelings such as the need to cry or laugh too much, or a sensation of anger or helplessness
- A decreased ability to think, causing the test-taker to blank out or have racing thoughts that are hard to organize or control.

Though most students will feel some level of anxiety when faced with a test or exam, the majority can cope with that anxiety and maintain it at a manageable level. However, those who cannot are faced with a very real and very serious condition, which can and should be controlled for the immeasurable benefit of this sufferer.

Naturally, these sensations lead to negative results for the testing experience. The most common effects of test anxiety have to do with nervousness and mental blocking.

Nervousness

Nervousness can appear in several different levels:

- The test-taker's difficulty, or even inability to read and understand the questions on the test
- The difficulty or inability to organize thoughts to a coherent form
- The difficulty or inability to recall key words and concepts relating to the testing questions (especially essays)
- The receipt of poor grades on a test, though the test material was well known by the test taker

Conversely, a person may also experience mental blocking, which involves:

- Blanking out on test questions
- Only remembering the correct answers to the questions when the test has already finished.

Fortunately for test anxiety sufferers, beating these feelings, to a large degree, has to do with proper preparation. When a test taker has a feeling of preparedness, then anxiety will be dramatically lessened.

The first step to resolving anxiety issues is to distinguish which of the two types of anxiety are being suffered. If the anxiety is a direct result of a lack of preparation, this should be considered a normal reaction, and the anxiety level (as opposed to the test results) shouldn't be anything to worry about. However, if, when adequately prepared, the test-taker still panics, blanks out, or seems to overreact, this is not a fully rational reaction. While this can be considered normal too, there are many ways to combat and overcome these effects.

Remember that anxiety cannot be entirely eliminated, however, there are ways to minimize it, to make the anxiety easier to manage. Preparation is one of the best ways to minimize test anxiety. Therefore the following techniques are wise in order to best fight off any anxiety that may want to build.

To begin with, try to avoid cramming before a test, whenever it is possible. By trying to memorize an entire term's worth of information in one day, you'll be shocking your system, and not giving yourself a very good chance to absorb the information. This is an easy path to anxiety, so for those who suffer from test anxiety, cramming should not even be considered an option.

Instead of cramming, work throughout the semester to combine all of the material which is presented throughout the semester, and work on it gradually as the course goes by, making sure to master the main concepts first, leaving minor details for a week or so before the test.

To study for the upcoming exam, be sure to pose questions that may be on the examination, to gauge the ability to answer them by integrating the ideas from your texts, notes and lectures, as well as any supplementary readings.

If it is truly impossible to cover all of the information that was covered in that particular term, concentrate on the most important portions, that can be covered very well. Learn these concepts as best as possible, so that when the test comes, a goal can be made to use these concepts as presentations of your knowledge.

In addition to study habits, changes in attitude are critical to beating a struggle with test anxiety. In fact, an improvement of the perspective over the entire test-taking experience can actually help a test taker to enjoy studying and therefore improve the overall experience. Be certain not to overemphasize the significance of the grade - know that the result of the test is neither a reflection of self worth, nor is it a measure of intelligence; one grade will not predict a person's future success.

To improve an overall testing outlook, the following steps should be tried:

- Keeping in mind that the most reasonable expectation for taking a test is to expect to try to demonstrate as much of what you know as you possibly can.
- Reminding ourselves that a test is only one test; this is not the only one, and there will be others.
- The thought of thinking of oneself in an irrational, all-or-nothing term should be avoided at all costs.
- A reward should be designated for after the test, so there's something to look forward to. Whether it be going to a movie, going out to eat, or simply visiting friends, schedule it in advance, and do it no matter what result is expected on the exam.

Test-takers should also keep in mind that the basics are some of the most important things, even beyond anti-anxiety techniques and studying. Never neglect the basic social, emotional and biological needs, in order to try to absorb information. In order to best achieve, these three factors must be held as just as important as the studying itself.

Study Steps

Remember the following important steps for studying:

- Maintain healthy nutrition and exercise habits. Continue both your recreational activities and social pass times. These both contribute to your physical and emotional well being.
- Be certain to get a good amount of sleep, especially the night before the test, because when you're overtired you are not able to perform to the best of your best ability.
- Keep the studying pace to a moderate level by taking breaks when they are needed, and varying the work whenever possible, to keep the mind fresh instead of getting bored.
- When enough studying has been done that all the material that can be learned has been learned, and the test taker is prepared for the test, stop studying and do something relaxing such as listening to music, watching a movie, or taking a warm bubble bath.

There are also many other techniques to minimize the uneasiness or apprehension that is experienced along with test anxiety before, during, or even after the examination. In fact, there are a great deal of things that can be done to stop anxiety from interfering with lifestyle and performance. Again, remember that anxiety will not be eliminated entirely, and it shouldn't be. Otherwise that "up" feeling for exams would not exist, and most of us depend on that sensation to perform better than usual. However, this anxiety has to be at a level that is manageable.

Of course, as we have just discussed, being prepared for the exam is half the battle right away. Attending all classes, finding out what knowledge will be expected on the exam, and knowing the exam schedules are easy steps to lowering anxiety. Keeping up with work will remove the need to cram, and efficient study habits will eliminate wasted time. Studying should be done in an ideal location for concentration, so that it is simple to become interested in the material and give it complete attention. A method such as SQ3R (Survey, Question, Read, Recite, Review) is a wonderful key to follow to make sure that the study habits are as effective as possible, especially in the case of learning from a textbook. Flashcards are great techniques for memorization. Learning to take good notes will mean that notes will be full of useful information, so that less sifting will need to be done to seek out what is pertinent for studying. Reviewing notes after class and then again on occasion will keep the information fresh in the mind. From notes that have been taken summary sheets and outlines can be made for simpler reviewing.

A study group can also be a very motivational and helpful place to study, as there will be a sharing of ideas, all of the minds can work together, to make sure that everyone understands, and the studying will be made more interesting because it will be a social occasion.

Basically, though, as long as the test-taker remains organized and self confident, with efficient study habits, less time will need to be spent studying, and higher grades will be achieved.

To become self confident, there are many useful steps. The first of these is "self talk." It has been shown through extensive research, that self-talk for students who suffer from test anxiety, should be well monitored, in order to make sure that it contributes to self confidence as opposed to sinking the student. Frequently the self talk of test-anxious students is negative or self-defeating, thinking that everyone else is smarter and faster, that they always mess up, and that if they don't do well, they'll fail the entire course. It is important to decreasing anxiety that awareness is made of self talk. Try writing any negative self thoughts and then disputing them with a positive statement instead. Begin self-encouragement as though it was a friend speaking. Repeat positive statements to help reprogram the mind to believing in successes instead of failures.

Helpful Techniques

Other extremely helpful techniques include:

- Self-visualization of doing well and reaching goals
- While aiming for an "A" level of understanding, don't try to "overprotect" by setting your expectations lower. This will only convince the mind to stop studying in order to meet the lower expectations.
- Don't make comparisons with the results or habits of other students. These are individual factors, and different things work for different people, causing different results.
- Strive to become an expert in learning what works well, and what can be done in order to improve. Consider collecting this data in a journal.
- Create rewards for after studying instead of doing things before studying that will only turn into avoidance behaviors.
- Make a practice of relaxing - by using methods such as progressive relaxation, self-hypnosis, guided imagery, etc - in order to make relaxation an automatic sensation.
- Work on creating a state of relaxed concentration so that concentrating will take on the focus of the mind, so that none will be wasted on worrying.
- Take good care of the physical self by eating well and getting enough sleep.
- Plan in time for exercise and stick to this plan.

Beyond these techniques, there are other methods to be used before, during and after the test that will help the test-taker perform well in addition to overcoming anxiety.

Before the exam comes the academic preparation. This involves establishing a study schedule and beginning at least one week before the actual date of the test. By doing this, the anxiety of not having enough time to study for the test will be automatically eliminated. Moreover, this will make the studying a much more effective experience, ensuring that the learning will be an easier process. This relieves much undue pressure on the test-taker.

Summary sheets, note cards, and flash cards with the main concepts and examples of these main concepts should be prepared in advance of the actual studying time. A topic should never be eliminated from this process. By omitting a topic because it isn't expected to be on the test is only setting up the test-taker for anxiety should it actually appear on the exam. Utilize the course syllabus for laying out the topics that should be studied. Carefully go over the notes that were made in class, paying special attention to any of the issues that the professor took special care to emphasize while lecturing in class. In the textbooks, use the chapter review, or if possible, the chapter tests, to begin your review.

It may even be possible to ask the instructor what information will be covered on the exam, or what the format of the exam will be (for example, multiple choice, essay, free form, true-false). Additionally, see if it is possible to find out how many questions will be on the test. If a review sheet or sample test has been offered by the professor, make good use of it, above anything else, for the preparation for the test. Another great resource for getting to know the examination is reviewing tests from previous semesters. Use these tests to review, and aim to achieve a 100% score on each of the possible topics. With a few exceptions, the goal that you set for yourself is the highest one that you will reach.

Take all of the questions that were assigned as homework, and rework them to any other possible course material. The more problems reworked, the more skill and confidence will form as a result. When forming the solution to a problem, write out each of the steps. Don't simply do head work. By doing as many steps on paper as possible, much clarification and therefore confidence will be formed. Do this with as many homework problems as possible, before checking the answers. By checking the answer after each problem, a reinforcement will exist, that will not be on the exam. Study situations should be as exam-like as possible, to prime the test-taker's system for the experience. By waiting to check the answers at the end, a psychological advantage will be formed, to decrease the stress factor.

Another fantastic reason for not cramming is the avoidance of confusion in concepts, especially when it comes to mathematics. 8-10 hours of study will become one hundred percent more effective if it is spread out over a week or at least several days, instead of doing it all in one sitting. Recognize that the human brain requires time in order to assimilate new material, so frequent breaks and a span of study time over several days will be much more beneficial.

Additionally, don't study right up until the point of the exam. Studying should stop a minimum of one hour before the exam begins. This allows the brain to rest and put things in their proper order. This will also provide the time to become as relaxed as possible when going into the examination room. The test-taker will also have time to eat well and eat sensibly. Know that the brain needs food as much as the rest of the body. With enough food and enough sleep, as well as a relaxed attitude, the body and the mind are primed for success.

Avoid any anxious classmates who are talking about the exam. These students only spread anxiety, and are not worth sharing the anxious sentimentalities.

Before the test also involves creating a positive attitude, so mental preparation should also be a point of concentration. There are many keys to creating a positive attitude. Should fears become rushing in, make a visualization of taking the exam, doing well, and seeing an A written on the paper. Write out a list of affirmations that will bring a feeling of confidence, such as "I am doing well in my English class," "I studied well and know my material," "I enjoy this class." Even if the affirmations aren't believed at first, it sends a positive message to the subconscious which will result in an alteration of the overall belief system, which is the system that creates reality.

If a sensation of panic begins, work with the fear and imagine the very worst! Work through the entire scenario of not passing the test, failing the entire course, and dropping out of school, followed by not getting a job, and pushing a shopping cart through the dark alley where you'll live. This will place things into perspective! Then, practice deep breathing and create a visualization of the opposite situation - achieving an "A" on the exam, passing the entire course, receiving the degree at a graduation ceremony.

On the day of the test, there are many things to be done to ensure the best results, as well as the most calm outlook. The following stages are suggested in order to maximize test-taking potential:

- Begin the examination day with a moderate breakfast, and avoid any coffee or beverages with caffeine if the test taker is prone to jitters. Even people who are used to managing caffeine can feel jittery or light-headed when it is taken on a test day.
- Attempt to do something that is relaxing before the examination begins. As last minute cramming clouds the mastering of overall concepts, it is better to use this time to create a calming outlook.
- Be certain to arrive at the test location well in advance, in order to provide time to select a location that is away from doors, windows and other distractions, as well as giving enough time to relax before the test begins.
- Keep away from anxiety generating classmates who will upset the sensation of stability and relaxation that is being attempted before the exam.
- Should the waiting period before the exam begins cause anxiety, create a self-distraction by reading a light magazine or something else that is relaxing and simple.

During the exam itself, read the entire exam from beginning to end, and find out how much time should be allotted to each individual problem. Once writing the exam, should more time be taken for a problem, it should be abandoned, in order to begin another problem. If there is time at the end, the unfinished problem can always be returned to and completed.

Read the instructions very carefully - twice - so that unpleasant surprises won't follow during or after the exam has ended.

When writing the exam, pretend that the situation is actually simply the completion of homework within a library, or at home. This will assist in forming a relaxed atmosphere, and will allow the brain extra focus for the complex thinking function.

Begin the exam with all of the questions with which the most confidence is felt. This will build the confidence level regarding the entire exam and will begin a quality momentum. This will also create encouragement for trying the problems where uncertainty resides.

Going with the "gut instinct" is always the way to go when solving a problem. Second guessing should be avoided at all costs. Have confidence in the ability to do well.

For essay questions, create an outline in advance that will keep the mind organized and make certain that all of the points are remembered. For multiple choice, read every answer, even if the correct one has been spotted - a better one may exist.

Continue at a pace that is reasonable and not rushed, in order to be able to work carefully. Provide enough time to go over the answers at the end, to check for small errors that can be corrected.

Should a feeling of panic begin, breathe deeply, and think of the feeling of the body releasing sand through its pores. Visualize a calm, peaceful place, and include all of the sights, sounds and sensations of this image. Continue the deep breathing, and take a few minutes to continue this with closed eyes. When all is well again, return to the test.

If a "blanking" occurs for a certain question, skip it and move on to the next question. There will be time to return to the other question later. Get everything done that can be done, first, to guarantee all the grades that can be compiled, and to build all of the confidence possible. Then return to the weaker questions to build the marks from there.

Remember, one's own reality can be created, so as long as the belief is there, success will follow. And remember: anxiety can happen later, right now, there's an exam to be written!

After the examination is complete, whether there is a feeling for a good grade or a bad grade, don't dwell on the exam, and be certain to follow through on the reward that was promised...and enjoy it! Don't dwell on any mistakes that have been made, as there is nothing that can be done at this point anyway.

Additionally, don't begin to study for the next test right away. Do something relaxing for a while, and let the mind relax and prepare itself to begin absorbing information again.

From the results of the exam - both the grade and the entire experience, be certain to learn from what has gone on. Perfect studying habits and work some more on confidence in order to make the next examination experience even better than the last one.

Learn to avoid places where openings occurred for laziness, procrastination and day dreaming.

Use the time between this exam and the next one to better learn to relax, even learning to relax on cue, so that any anxiety can be controlled during the next exam. Learn how to relax the body. Slouch in your chair if that helps. Tighten and then relax all of the different muscle groups, one group at a time, beginning with the feet and then working all the way up to the neck and face. This will ultimately relax the muscles more than they were to begin with. Learn how to breathe deeply and comfortably, and focus on this breathing going in and out as a relaxing thought. With every exhale, repeat the word "relax."

As common as test anxiety is, it is very possible to overcome it. Make yourself one of the test-takers who overcome this frustrating hindrance.

Additional Bonus Material

Due to our efforts to try to keep this book to a manageable length, we've created a link that will give you access to all of your additional bonus material.

Please visit http://www.mometrix.com/bonus948/gaphyssci to access the information.